Going the Extra Mile

DANIEL SEDDIQUI

Dedication

To my wife, Holly, during the world
pandemic, for not putting our lives on hold
and inspiring me to get things done.

To all the people in this book, thank
you for sharing your lives.

Contents

Prologue

"Curiosity propels action, a window to learn and an opportunity for progress"

Heading west down Interstate-90, just before crossing over the Missouri River in South Dakota, I spotted a sign "Indian Reservation -50 miles." I had never been to a reservation, let alone meet a Native American. I was curious.

Hearing a National Public Radio segment on obesity in America's food deserts, where kids became so large that in Mississippi the size of school buses had to widen. I was curious.

Patrolling the border of Arizona, catching dozens of undocumented immigrants coming through the sewer systems, my boss states, "often, they're coming here for a better life." I had wondered what kinds of jobs they find and how they live under the radar. I was curious.

Driving with my employer in Kentucky's horse country, during my initial American journey of working 50 Jobs in 50 States in 50 Weeks, he pointed out a trailer home down by the river. "You should see the way people live in the Eastern part of the state of Appalachia," he suggested. I was curious.

Riding the Chicago "L" train through the southside of the city, police lights blaring block after block, I heard that some neighborhoods are so dangerous that bullets can fly into your bedroom while you're sleeping. I was curious.

I felt like I've seen it all, after traveling to every state in America to work in just as many industries. Going deep in the coal mines of West Virginia, pulling up lobster traps off the coast of Maine, plunging a soil sampler probe in the fields of Iowa and pressing grapes from the iconic vineyards of Napa Valley, my curiosity kept growing with each experience. And, if I forget about the experience, it's the people I've met that made the biggest impression on me. I wanted to continue learning about people, no matter who they are, what they are or where they're from. That's the greatness of America. The diversity. It's an endless Wikipedia page, an infinite google search with no margins.

Unfortunately, the country is not all rainbows and butterflies. On the contrary, my curiosity had led me to discover the many problems we've swept under the rug, especially in places that have become separate societies that many are unaware. I decided to "drop in" to the communities that have been hit the hardest, to put myself into the shoes of others and learn how epidemics develop in each place. For one month in each of the 5 regions of America, I was curious to visit the Mississippi Delta to focus on obesity, Pine Ridge

Reservation's high unemployment and its byproduct, South Chicago's gun violence, Appalachia's extreme poverty, and Central California's immigration.

I was born curious, and it's what I decide to do with it that matters. I know this would be a humbling journey, one that I hope sparks curiosity and respect of one another.

We're Still Here–
Pine Ridge

I'm stranded in the parking lot on the Pine Ridge Indian Reservation in South Dakota. Stray dogs are circling my rental car and I'm not sure on how to react. I can't drive away because one of them is under the car. They're big dogs with discolored eyes, warts like cow utters underneath their frame, and ears bitten off. Either they're seeking shade from the blistering sun or looking for attention from me. I've been questioning what do to for the last fifteen minutes, after realizing that I'm late for my meeting with the principal of a federally funded private high school.

I left Denver on a familiar route on my way to a place that was very foreign. Before leaving, I called Chuck Mills—the nephew of Billy Mills, who was a Native American that came out of nowhere to win the 1964 Olympic gold medal in the 10,000-meter event

I met Chuck through his work at the Denver Indian Center, where he helps Natives who have been recently released from prison get jobs. By providing them with free gas and gift cards, the center gives them incentives to keep working. He sounded pessimistic and felt that the government was dumping a lot of money into programs like his. I was gathering information and didn't want to make any rushed judgements, but it seemed like one way or another, the government was paying for the lives of the Natives, so better it's in a way that's productive and aims towards self-sufficiency.

I was a little concerned leading up to my trip to Pine Ridge, but Chuck made me even more nervous. Though he was born on the reservation, Chuck mentioned he doesn't feel welcome when he visits. "They call me 'apple': red on the outside and white on the inside." He told me about the deadliest two mile stretch in the world, gangs killing random people, the young preying on the elderly. I couldn't help worrying I was stumbling into hell on a suicide mission.

Chuck asked me my intentions, suggesting that the only reason Whites (e.g. Non-Natives) come to the reservation is to make a change, which is completely rejected by the locals; the last thing they want is help from the White man. "If you're going there just to be you and learn about the way of life, then they're the warmest people," Chuck said. I wasn't quite sure how I would need to act to ensure they'd find me to be genuine—after all, I was entering a different culture, where even Chuck didn't feel accepted. He later explained that with all the tribes, cultures, and philosophies, the Native American people are more diverse than Europeans.

Our conversation made me start to rethink this social study, but it also sparked my curiosity, and motivated me to discover if I could gain the acceptance of the community I'd be entering. Chuck told me that I'd be alright if I'm upfront, honest and genuine with the Native people. If not, I'd be run out of town real fast.

Before making the trip, I looked up some pictures of the Pine Ridge Reservation on the internet and forwarded them to my mom. She told me I wouldn't last a day; I believed her. My dad thought the Natives would beat me up for fun, with nothing to lose. I was full of dread, but I knew I needed to pursue this. As they say, curiosity kills the cat.

On my drive through the vastness of Wyoming and Western Nebraska, parts of the state could be mistaken for Reservation land. The only difference being these towns were populated with White people, but now that I'm getting closer to South Dakota's Pine Ridge, I'm scared.

In 2008, when I took off for my journey of *50 Jobs in 50 States*, I had gone through similar emotions, but I had an early sense of comfort staying with my Uncle Mike in Utah when I began that trip. Without that, I may never have had the courage to start. Working *50 Jobs* brought me to South Dakota for the first time, and it was there I met the White family (I know, what a coincidence for a last name). They lived on the Southwestern part of the state in the cowboy town of Oelrichs, population 124. Oelrichs is just fifteen miles from the border of the reservation.

On this trip, the White family gave me the same early comfort as Uncle Mike had years before. They were just as welcoming as when we first met. Their daughters, Ellen and Brenda even offered a spare bedroom for the month in their home. It made me think back to Chuck's question, *are you going cold turkey?* Because of the White family, I would say warm turkey.

My first night in Oelrichs felt like the calm before the storm. I walked around the grass fields with the daughters and their cute dogs. You could see as far as the eye can see. We talked about how harsh the weather and wildfires had been. "You can notice a fire coming our direction 60 miles from our house." The joke out there is that you could spot a bad person coming miles away. Out in the summer, lightning can ignite fires out here, and it's so desolate, there's seemingly no escape from the flames. Just about every community member in these small towns serves as a volunteer firefighter. They get no media attention, so the rest of the country will have no idea what comes and goes in this region. It's easy to forget an area this isolated and just about every Reservation is on undesirable land.

I had researched places to work with youth on the Reservation, focusing on addressing the highest unemployment statistic in the nation: 80–90%. I wanted to learn how a community could live without working and what challenges their youth faced. Ellen, the eldest daughter of the White family, threw me some suggestions. She and her younger sister, Brenda, are both elementary teachers on the Reservation. They teach reading and writing, which are the toughest subjects for Native kids. I told them that I'd been in contact with a youth program director on Facebook, but hadn't heard from her in weeks, despite getting in touch months ago about my trip. I asked if I could come join them at their schools.

"We'll ask the principal tomorrow," Ellen optimistically responded.

We hopped into their car and drove three blocks down a dirt road to the local bar and grill, one of the two places to eat in town. It had a huge mural of a Native American man on the side. It looked majestic, despite the paint fading.

"The owners are planning to take that down and it's probably going to rustle some feathers," Brenda said.

The majestic Indian Mural has been threatened to be removed by the Oelrichs Bar & Grill owner.

Of course, I wanted to go into the restaurant. Inside, only one customer was there chatting with the bartender/owner. They were both White, which I expected. I started talking to them about my visit to the reservation. I mentioned that I heard on the radio that liquor store owners in Whiteclay, Nebraska would immorally take advantage of the Natives by selling alcohol right outside the dry reservation limits. Thirty minutes into our conversation, the same customer turned to me and told me she was Indian. I hadn't expected it and realized I could've met a Native before and wouldn't have known. With her biker-type outfit, she seemed to have assimilated well in Oelrichs. She told me to refer to Natives as Indians since that's how the locals identify themselves.

As two people walked in the bar with dark clothing, my heart stopped and I felt the bar fall silent. I wasn't sure how or why the bar got silent, and maybe it was only in my mind. It was a man and a woman, but I doubted that the woman was Indian – she came in with an 80s rock look that reminded me of Joan Jett: big hair and lots of dark makeup. When they entered, you could see on their faces that they didn't know why we were all looking at them. The guy wore a trucker hat, but his features were distinctly Indian, almost resembling the mural.

I watched as the man casually bought a beer, and I couldn't help but stare at the money he exchanged with the bartender. I wondered how he got it, and how much of it he had. I had so many questions about reparations. After five minutes of toying with a casino-arcade game, he disappeared. When we finally left the bar ourselves, I spotted him sitting in the back room at a slot machine. At the same moment, a man with a cowboy hat walked in and said hello to me. The sun shone right on his stately face, and it was a young Indian. In my mind, they were celebrities, just as any persons with such different backgrounds from my own, like the Amish or preppy Southerners. I just wanted to shake their hands. This was the first true exposure to Natives in my entire life, and we were not yet on the reservation, but I left truly analyzing if the reservation should reconsider its policy of being dry. If the reservation permitted buying and selling alcohol, Natives would bring or keep money in their own community, rather than coming fifteen or more miles to towns like Oelrichs to buy a drink. I was eager to explore Whiteclayat some point during this endeavor. I'd heard it was the epitome of human greed and corruption with four liquor stores in a town of fourteen residents, and those businesses generate over three million dollars per year. It's located just on the other side of the dry reservation.

Later that night, Brenda and Ellen drove me thirty-five miles to Chadron, Nebraska, where they get all their shopping done, just as Indians do on the first of the month. We went grocery shopping at Walmart to stock up for the week. Then we sat in the car as it crawled through a McDonald's drive-thru for forty minutes, instead of walking into the restaurant. It seemed like a culture, where your car was your mobility. I pondered the idea that one could become a product of his/ her environment, and how we become just like those around us. The car in front of us had a party of five, and I noticed they were Indians. Kids in diapers were crawling around the car, and trash was piled against the back window. Instead of ordering at McDonalds, I opted to get a sandwich at the grocery store and mentioned to the young teenage cashier that I'm headed to Pine Ridge. She had a look on her face like a ghost went through her. "Be careful!"

The next morning, I said my farewells to the Whites and headed out early for the reservation. Along the drive was such vastness. I didn't know much about reservations. I always figured there would be areas that catered to tourists, to explore historical grounds and learn about the Native people. I thought there would be teepees to stay in, or places to watch pow-wows. And of course, the casinos. I had never connected the dots of a history of people being displaced and shoved in the most isolated, unusable parts of the country. I wasn't prepared to be this far disconnected in such remoteness.

The saying, "you can see a bad person coming from miles away" rang in my head.

The long descend to the Pine Ridge Reservation of South Dakota.

Ten miles down into the valley, I spotted a large wooden sign, *Welcome to The Pine Ridge Reservation*. I was still out in the open, with nothing to see but prairie fields. I got out of the car and set up my camera for a selfie in front of yet another welcome sign. This had become a tradition from my *50 Jobs* venture when entering a new state.

I was headed to central Pine Ridge, but for some reason, things got in my way on the drive; small birds fly from the roadside shrubs, stray dogs crossing the road like deer, locals walking along the highway, and then I stumbled into a protest in the intersection of "town". Indians wearing bandanas, riding horses and holding flags. I wasn't sure what they were protesting, but if it was a national issue, I doubted they would ever be heard.

I could barely find parking outside the government offices of Oglala Sioux Tribe, where I was tracking down my only contact, Sammi Gordon. She's the youth program director of the Workforce Investment Act (WIA), which provides youth an opportunity for career development and exploration—my specialty. I found her on Facebook and had several conversations with her about coming to help her Indian youth.

I stepped out of my car into July's oppressive 110°F temperature and walked towards the entrance of the building, past a sign that said to keep the doors closed to prevent flies from entering. Flyswatters hung on the walls—flies were obviously a huge problem in this part of the country. A huge fan blew at the entrance, keeping the hot outdoor air and flies from coming in. Passing through the halls of the building and I saw the door for an employment services office. Lots of job postings were on the walls advertising labor intensive work.

I asked the Indian receptionist, "Are these job postings for Natives only?"

"No, these are for anyone on the reservation."

"How come the unemployment is so high, even with all these job postings?" I asked.

"Either nobody wants to work, it's hard to get to, or specific skills are needed," she replied. To me, the jobs advertised were very basic, like janitorial or office clerk. I wondered if there was a larger issue and that's what brought me here. I walked down the basement stairs to the WIA office, where I was supposed to find Sammi. A young man was sitting at a conference table.

"Do you know where I can find Sammi?" I asked.

"She's not here, she's at the arena," he said curtly.

I had a feeling that this was going to be a cat and mouse game, and nobody wanted to help me. It was obvious, I wasn't wanted there or possibly, the communication skills are weak, and why I heard that progress was slow on the reservation. I went to the arena looking for Sammi, and interrupted a male counselor playing with a group of kids. The counselor told me, "She's at the government office."

"I was just there and was told to find her here."

"Let me try her on her cell phone." The counselor left her a message; just like I had done for the past ten days. It was becoming clearer that I was being avoided.

I hesitantly returned to the WIA office, where I met the young man, Matt for the second time. It turned out he was the co-director of the youth program and he was not excited to see me again. He was wondering who the hell I was.

After all I had gone through to get to the reservation, I wasn't going to walk away without the opportunity of working here—especially when it was right in front of me. Nothing worth it, is ever easy.

I had to get this done. I had to sell myself. I was tired of the constant awkwardness.

"Sorry for being such a nuisance," I said. "Can I tell you my situation, Matt? I was invited here by Sammi and I haven't heard from her in weeks. I came from Colorado voluntarily and wanted to work with your team."

Matt suggested that I come back the next day, and he would find a role for me on such short notice.

I went back in my car to cruise around the nearby neighborhood. One street had a row of nonprofits, including several addiction treatment centers. I spotted non-Natives names as directors of the offices. I heard a middle-aged Indian man walking out of a treatment center cheering, "I'm going to be back on my feet." On the radio, I listened to local rap music as I drove past a water tower tagged with gang graffiti. It's not a place I expected inner city culture to take place, but by the week's end, I learned that the youth was heavily influenced by that culture. Many teenage Indians dressed as if they were in a hip-hop music video and to further that stereotype, basketball is a major pastime.

Knowing that I wasn't going to make much progress with my work, I used the free time to continue exploring. I wanted to see the deadliest two mile stretch of the world that Chuck mentioned, and it was staring at me like the barrel of a gun. A road sign read: White Clay 2. From the gas station in the center of Pine Ridge's business district to the border of Nebraska was just a stone's throw. I turned on my video camera and started recording. I drove past lines of Indians walking on the side of the road. Memorials in the trenches of the grass proved this wasn't a place of myth. I decided to turn off the camera and focus on the oncoming traffic. With every car passing on the two-lane road, I was ready to veer off the road if I needed to avoid oncoming traffic. Any driver could've been under the influence. I sped up when there were no cars, just to get the drive over with. When I arrived in White Clay, it was worse than I expected. Because the liquor stores made so much money, I had assumed they would be modern, plush, and attractive for customers. I didn't dare to leave my car to walk in. I was fine just observing the flow of activity from my car.

It was one of the ugliest scenes I had witnessed in the country. Men and women were laying on the sidewalk, underneath the scarcity of shade. I learned that none of the stores had restrooms. The liquor stores didn't want people spending time in their shops; they only wanted people to come in, make a purchase, and leave.

I drove back to the reservation, where I imagined the route of bootlegging occurs. Back in the center of town, I had wondered if these treatment centers didn't do enough in terms of outreach, but then again, Chuck reminded me that Indians refuse help from the White man. I remembered watching Diane Sawyer's special about this reservation that featured an alcoholic treatment center. I wanted to go and meet the woman that was interviewed. I couldn't bank on working at the WIA office. So, I used my smartphone to look up Eileen Janis, the woman featured in that special, and called her office. No one answered.

I decided to drive to the center, located in Kyle, because I wanted to explore a new town on the reservation. When I checked the map, it looked like a long route, because it was indirect; it was up to a town, over a town, onto another town, and I just decided to go for it. I had the extra time, and when else could I do it?

In happenstance, I drove through a town called "Wounded Knee," a historic landmark and site of a tragic battle between Lakota Indians and the U.S. army. I saw two men selling jewelry on the side of the road and decided to stop to finally get a chance to speak to more locals. As I approached their jewelry, I spotted beautiful earrings that were shaped like a net. I asked what the net represented, and one man said that it was to catch evil. I bought the earrings and climbed back into my car. I drove to the next town, called "Porcupine," and found a post office. I decided I would mail the earrings to my fiancé, there and then. I was eager to hear what she thought of receiving a package from me from so far away on a reservation—a unique experience for both of us.

I trekked on to Kyle, South Dakota, where I found the Anpetu Luta Otipi Alcoholic Treatment Center—the same center featured on the Diane Sawyer segment. I went into the office and knocked on the door; it was a beautiful facility! Inside was modern, I assumed because it was subsidized by the federal government. A secretary opened the door for me.

"Is the celebrity here?" I asked.

"You mean Eileen?

"The one featured on Diane Sawyer's segment."

"Oh, she's not in," she replied. "She's at a Sun Dance."

"I'm only here for a short period of time; can I get in touch with her before I leave? I came all the way from Colorado," I pleaded.

She rang Eileen on her cell phone. My head almost exploded with excitement.

"Hi Eileen, there's a gentleman here who wants to meet you and get your autograph," she said, before passing me the phone.

I wasn't sure where the conversation would lead, but it was the biggest window into their culture. "I am at a Sun Dance, you are welcome to come and meet me here," Eileen said, before giving me directions to meet her. "Go South to Allen, B1A4, Bondocks 18, head into Batesland, and then you'll come to a road, Gordon Junction; left on the gravel road." I couldn't even write the directions because they sounded so foreign to me. Eileen gave me her cell phone number and we hung up. I went over the directions a second time with her secretary.

As expected, I was still completely lost during the drive. I found two men sitting outside of their driveway. I asked them directions and they asked me, "Do you have a buck?" I said no, and they told me to get lost.

I had to take guesses in so many places. There was a point where I found Gordon Junction, but saw nothing there but a house. I parked on the side of the road and took out my phone to call Eileen; just my luck, there was no cell phone service. I wasn't sure if I should knock on a stranger's door, so I decided to just keep guessing. I found the dirt road and had to open a gate to bring my car through. Three miles later, I saw another gate on a long, private, dirt road and there it was: at least 300 trucks parked in a dirt lot. I'd found it. I was finally at the Sun Dance.

I didn't recall what Eileen looked like from her television appearance, so I left it up to her to find me. I walked around the grounds, completely obtrude before someone called my name. There was Eileen, as pleasant as a ray of sunshine.

When I walked up to greet her, she seemed happy to see me. Her warm welcome was a surprise and felt great after making no progress with any other contacts on the reservation thus far. Eileen introduced me to her niece and a few others in passing. Most people were spectators at the Sun Dance, but everyone there was Indian.

As I looked around me, I saw sweat lodges. Eileen explained that the "sacrificers," (also known as the sun dancers) stay in the dome shaped hut in excruciating temperatures for two weeks.

"What's the purpose?" I asked.

"The Sun Dance is a ritual of sacrifice and purification," Eileen explained. "You make yourself suffer to the point where pain is not of significance."

As the Sun Dance progressed, Eileen continued to explain the tradition. I saw a long, twenty-five-foot pole in the middle of the dirt lot. There were long ropes attached to the pole, with a nail at the end of each rope. I learned later, that this was preparation before the true sacrifice was made. A lot of the Indians had beer guts, and I wondered if they were sacrificing at the Sun Dance because they had overcome their alcoholism, or some other rock bottom realization prompted a drastic change for a new life.

It's hard for a young person to fight against the grain of external forces. As I learned earlier, many young Indians are into American pop culture and neglect their traditional heritage. That all began decades ago, when reservations were first established and young Indians were kidnapped by White people—taken from their homes and their lands—and brought to new territory to forget about their culture, their language, and their families. As a result, there's a constant struggle to bring the Indian heritage back. In private schools, there are classes about the culture for thirty minutes each week, which aren't offered in public schools. Kids today find it easier to fall into negativity, like gangs, suicide, and dropping out of school, when at one time, kids were brought up to endure pain as part of their spirituality.

Eileen explained, "kids are scared to embrace our traditional religion because it's too powerful."

It wouldn't be long before I learned what the nail at the end of each rope connected to the tall pole was used for. The participants would insert the nail underneath their skin. Then, they would fall back and let their skin rip from their body, as blood would drip from their skin, creating permanent scars. If you ever see an Indian with intense scarring on their upper back or chest, you will know they made the great sacrifice for their beliefs. During a long intermission, I decided it was time to thank Eileen and head out. I didn't want to overstay my welcome. I asked to stay in touch with her if I had more questions, and Eileen graciously gave me her email address and added me on Facebook.

As I was leaving, Eileen's niece, Brittany, asked me for a ride to Pine Ridge. I was surprised that she would trust a stranger to drive her over fifteen miles to the next town, because we'd barely said hello. I agreed to give her a lift.

"My mom was supposed to show up, but she's drunk," Brittany blurted out as we drove away. Brittany was nineteen, mother of a two-year-old child, and more experienced than most people her age.

As we rode back, she told me about her life, almost as if I was her psychologist. Ten minutes into our car ride, Brittany admitted that she had attempted suicide. I found that to be very common on the reservation—even billboards on the reservation addressed the issue—but now I saw the statistic in the passenger seat of my car. Before hearing Brittany's story, I assumed someone would commit suicide only based on their own sense of hopelessness and depression. I learned that Brittany was hopeful and confident in herself, but she had been overwhelmed with the burdens of those around her.

Brittany's ex-boyfriend was an alcoholic and was abusive toward her. He had been deployed to Iraq for 7 months but got kicked out of the military. Her mom was partying, drinking every night, and not providing for the family. Brittany's dad passed away when she was twelve, and after that she was the only person in her family working and supporting her mother and siblings. The stress was insurmountable, and Brittany had attempted to slit her wrists. Brittany was at the Sun Dance because she was trying to take her aunt's advice to hang around righteous people. It had been Brittany's first time at a Sun Dance, not just mine.

As we drove into town and spotted kids riding horses bareback, thoughts had constantly gone through my mind about people who live on the reservation and if they've had the sense of the outside world.

"Have you ever left the reservation?" I asked Brittany.

"Yes; I lived in Sioux Falls, SD, but that didn't last long," she replied. "I went to attend school, and I felt like everything was as I expected. I paid for everything without assistance. I enjoyed living in a city and I was focusing on a career, but family dysfunction called me back. That's what brings most of us back – our family, and our tradition. Unfortunately, not many of us follow our tradition any longer."

Pop culture has taken over the reservation—typical pop culture you'd see anywhere in America. What surprised me more than anything was the inner-city-like gangs you'd find in Chicago or Los Angeles. Through my exploratory drives on Pine Ridge, I saw so much gang graffiti on water towers, on office buildings; there even came a point when I saw an old Cadillac with hydraulics on a dirt road. Unbelievable!

Brittany told me about her new boyfriend, Jacob. They went to school together, and Brittany told me that he would try to compete with her over their life's struggles, though his hardships were nothing close to hers.

I brought Brittany to her destination: the gas station right in the center of town. I appreciated our time together. It was good getting to know a local on the reservation.

The next day I went back to see Matt. Once again, he didn't want to make eye contact with me. I sat patiently, waiting for the "team" to come, but over an hour later, I was still sitting there with Matt.

"What's going on? Where is everybody?" I asked.

"They should have been here," he replied. I wasn't surprised by the lack of diligence in the program, but I was disappointed that a government run program was being managed the way it was.

I asked Matt a few questions about himself and was surprised when he was willing to chat. I had never met people who were so open with their personal struggles. Matt started drinking at an early age. He married at seventeen and continued drinking until he had his own kid. He didn't know of a single family unaffected by drugs and alcohol on the reservation. (I later found that 85% of families on the reservation are affected by alcohol).

Matt was now a product of the WIA program and had earned a Bill Gates Scholarship to attend college. He went to the University of New Mexico to study psychology so he could help people in similar situations as his. It is common for people to return to Pine Ridge and help the community.

I realized that there are a couple of ways to approach the federal government's philosophy behind establishing the reservations. On the one hand, you could say that the government is trying to make up for its tragic history with the Natives by giving them land and funding as a gift. On the other hand, you could consider that the government is trying to isolate the Natives and gives them funding to suppress and remove them from the rest of society.

The government could provide meaningful assistance to the Natives, like helping them find ways to invest in their own communities or to overcome the problems of alcoholism. Instead, the government will give money to individuals who are not working, which becomes a disincentive for people to look for work. A job can not only provide an income, but can help people find a sense of purpose, a social outlet, and meaning to their lives. Without jobs, people waste their days and have more destructive behavior. So, in a sense, the free handouts that the government provided the Natives were actually holding them down.

I heard a local news channel that continuously recited job openings with locations and pay rates, eager to find people to fill positions. Yet, as I found stopping by the employment services office, the biggest issue in Indian unemployment is they cannot find people who are sober to work.

Three hours later, Matt received a call from Alicia, who runs the youth job placement program. She agreed to have me assist her for a week. Alicia was hosting students from the town of Oglala. She would be conducting an initiation meeting for the seventeen teenagers in the Workforce Investment Program.

I took off immediately to meet her. Once I thought I had arrived, I wanted to make sure I was in the right place, so I asked a student wearing a t-shirt saying *we gonna light this rez up,* "Are you in WIA?" but he said no. I felt like he was trying to brush me off. I still walked in the room, and saw it filled with depressed looking kids, like it was a funeral. The students obviously did not want to be there.

I picked up a program from the table, listing the rules of the curriculum.

To participate, students must qualify as being below the federal poverty line; those who do not qualify have to drive farther and find their own jobs. For this reason, the program is essential.

Students must be between fourteen and twenty-one years old. They must work a minimum of 4 hours per day, for four weeks. They are paid $7.25 per hour. The program is run in three counties, nine districts, and 52 communities.

There are not many choices for work on the reservation. There are just four main industries. One is the school system. Another is the hospital, where you'll find most non-natives working as doctors and nurses. The third is the casino, where business is so slow that I found a security officer lying on the couch. The last option is tribal affairs, which is typically reserved for the elite. There are a couple of corner stores as well. Alicia's primary role is to place the students to these facilities.

I sat quietly in the corner, trying to go unnoticed, waiting for Alicia to show up to the morning meeting. We waited over twenty minutes, so I walked to the next building, the college center, to look for Alicia. I think I spotted Alicia sitting at a receptionist desk. She got up and walked past me.

"Are you Alicia?" and she shook my hand and walked back to her timecards against the wall. A girl gets close to Alicia, as I assumed it was her assistant.

"Are you Alicia's assistant? Are we going to the room with the kids?" She was outright rude and ignored me. I held the door open for her, and she said nothing. Nobody, not even the staff, looked like they wanted to be there.

Alicia has a doctorate in clinical psychology and has always wanted to go into school counseling and teaching. Once we got to know each other, she and I actually got along well because we had lots in common – for one, we both wanted to help youth in career development.

After the informational meeting, we headed to another facility as a large group. I tried to make conversation with a young girl, but she did not even turn her head to acknowledge me. It was clear that she was ignoring me – but I couldn't let that get to me.

While Alicia did paperwork, I asked if I could give a presentation. I thought it might break the ice with the students.

"What do you want to present? she asked.

"I can talk about career exploration based on my *50 jobs* journey that I mentioned to you about." She looked at some open dates and told me that I could present at the end of the week. Until then, I'd have to put up with being ignored.

I got back into my car and turned on the local radio station: KILI. It had a great mix of genres, from drumming and chanting to pop and hip-hop. I listened to a local girl sing "Amazing Grace," and I heard a rock song that crooned, "red people are our people." The DJ was an amateur but made me laugh. "To all you brown people out there," he said, "stay positive and happy!"

I kept the radio on KILI when it transferred to a national Indian station based in Albuquerque. *Two Dudes with Good Moods* came on to talk about their comedy stardom, from alcohol to the turning point of celebrity. I decided to call in – what had I got to lose?

"I'm a non-native on Pine Ridge, believe it or not," I said.

"Oh, I believe it!"

"What advice do you have for those who need to find their purpose, like you guys did?"

"It's easy to be negative," they explained. "There are many reasons to be upset and angry. But it feels better to be positive and help others. We are all role models. Might as well be positive ones. Indians are traditionally warriors, not the fighting you think, but to protect your family and your people. It's important to be a part of the world and not in isolation. Women out there, a true woman, respects herself." They went on and on, the two dudes with good moods, being totally serious and not saying anything humorous at all. It made me think about how important it is to live life with purpose. As they said, "everybody has a spirit." That's something I wanted to incorporate into my presentation.

The following day, I went to the college center where WIA would meet, and where I would be giving a PowerPoint presentation. I was anxious to see how the audience would respond to my message, experience, and presence. I have given similar talks around the country, but there was no setting like a reservation. The challenges these students face are not like others face. The environment they live in is something I've been learning about each day.

As I gave my presentation, the audience seemed engaged and attentive; but my goal was to learn about the people, dig into their thoughts and aspirations, and understand if they felt limited on the reservation. I had created a questionnaire, administered by WIA, with five simple questions. After all, I came to the reservation to learn and make a difference, and the questionnaire was the most strategic way to get the students to open up to me.

At the end of the presentation, I offered a free book to any student that had a great question. To my surprise, the student that looked least interested in my presentation was excited to receive my book. I took a picture with her. I will cherish that moment, because it was the first time I felt a connection with an Indian youth, the first time I didn't feel like a stranger, the first time being genuinely accepted.

I collected the questionnaires and learned more about the students based on their answers. First, I had asked students to name their dream job. Most students wanted to be a teacher, or to work in a sports related career. I asked students what work means to them and found that most students are focused on earning money, and only want to work to earn a living wage.

I had asked the students to define what was important to them, and many students said that family and friends were most important. One student wrote that it was most important to find a job "so I will stop worrying."

It made my heart heavy that the students' greatest concerns involved financial stability. That the students carried such a burden of worry to feed their families seemed extraordinary, while most teenagers across the country worry about clothes and dating. After reading the questionnaires, I felt like I understood the kids better and was inspired to work with them. This is when my curiosity turned to compassion.

That afternoon, Eileen reached out to me to see if I would be interested in attending a feather ceremony. Just like the sun dance opportunity, I jumped on the offer to attend. I met Eileen at a luncheon to celebrate her daughter's friend, Mona, who had just graduated from a college in Washington DC. At the party, I was welcomed with the smiling faces of a crowd ecstatic and proud of Mona's accomplishment. I also met Mona, who was very kind and excited to partake in the tradition of putting a feather in her hair.

As I was sitting and chatting with Eileen and her friends, I talked about my experience with WIA and the youth I was working with.

"How are the students treating you?" Eileen asked.

"They hadn't talked to me much," I replied.

Eileen laughed. "They are going to test you, that's the reality," she explained. I was relieved to know that the students' demeanor toward me was to be expected. Eileen continued. "I feel like an outsider sometimes myself. I get invited to events, such as this, but I don't fit in because I don't have the baggage many others do. I don't even know my neighbors anymore," she lamented.

As she spoke, we heard the master of ceremonies calling for prayer as the feather ceremony began. We gathered solemnly and respectfully in a circle around the man who was chanting. I wasn't sure how long the chanting would last. It seemed to go on for an eternity, though it only lasted twenty minutes. Ultimately, I was honored to be a part of the experience, thanks to Eileen.

Eileen Janis saying a few word(s) about her friend's daughter before her traditional feather ceremony at a local community center.

When the weekend finally came, I decided to visit my old friend Brad an hour away in Rapid City. I met him the same week as the White family, during my *50 jobs* trip. He's a small business owner that makes custom Cowboy hats. Considering he was born and raised in South Dakota, I wanted to get his impression of the reservation, and see what perspective he could share with me.

It was clear that Brad didn't want the reservation to exist and wanted the Indians to be integrated in other cities. Brad felt that the Indians were relying on others and doing less for themselves. He felt the issues on reservations were self-inflicted wounds. Rather than building a grocery store to shop in on their own land, he complained, Indians built a new casino that got no business. Brad also mentioned that Indians lease their land to be farmed by outsiders. He told me to look at any of the roads on the reservation and notice that all of them seem to be under construction. Brad felt that instilling the dignity of work and pride could be a huge remedy for their plight.

I started back down to Oelrichs for the night. It was getting dark and the clouds were moving fast. Across the open horizon, I spotted lightning in the distance. As I was drove, the storm closed in on me. Suddenly a lightning bolt struck right on the road in front of me, lighting up the pavement! I immediately turned around, went to a parking lot, and tried to wait it out. I sat there for over an hour, but the storm did not ease up. I called the White family and told them I would be late because of lightning, but they only laughed. "Don't worry—you have rubber tires," they explained. "You will be immune to any harm from the lightning."

The next work week started, and I was off and running—planning jobs, monitoring positions, and helping students with disciplinary professionalism. I was placing kids in jobs at nursing homes, at the local convenience store, helping to build houses, and at local daycares. I wanted students to see the value of any experience, even if it wasn't their dream job. The biggest lesson is to gain a sense of identity and develop skills for the next steps in life. Although money is a huge driving factor, I wanted the kids to understand that purpose was more important, just as the *Two Dudes in Good Moods* had proven. "Find something you're good at and go for it, even if it doesn't make you a living – find that purpose."

Two weeks into working with the students, my biggest hope was for them to see a world outside of their ordinary life and to aspire to some career avenues that weren't immediately apparent. It was a work in progress, but when my time on the reservation was up, I decided to get some insights from the principal of the private high school that had the stray dogs circling my rental car, called Red Cloud Indian School.

"We are an unemployment society. People here work for two weeks at a time just to earn a paycheck to drink. We are fighting a lot of external forces with our kids, and since this new school opened in 2010, we are making major progress. We have the best facilities," the principal explained, as she gave me a tour of the science lab. "In 1990, only 19% of high school kids went to college. In 2010, at our school, we have 100% of our kids graduate. We have many of our alumni return to serve as mentors and visit with our students to help guide them, even if it's off the reservation. We do have traumatic events still – one of our students committed suicide just last week, but I am hopeful to keep kids involved and driven and help our neighbors."

As I drove off the reservation and back to Oelrichs for the final time, I was encouraged – I passed a kid standing in his driveway, waiting for his bus, reading a book.

Labor of Love

I was cruising in my Jeep, the same vehicle that I used for *50 Jobs in 50 States*—yes, my Jeep and I were embarking on yet another journey together. I went along the produce fields in central California. This is a part of the state where you'll find the produce 'capitals' of fruit, vegetables and nuts— roadside stands with huge colorful handmade billboards calling to passing interstate drivers. As I drove, I was looking for work.

Finding work as a field hand turned out to be a more difficult prospect than I'd expected. Fieldworkers are often day laborers, having to migrate from field to field, across the region. I figured I'd do the same.

I drove forty-five miles to Watsonville, the 'Strawberry Capital', where Driscoll's Berries is located, to get work as a field hand. I had made several phone calls to confirm that they were hiring before making the drive. There was even a posting on the job board of the United Farm Workers website.

I showed up to the Driscoll offices, which consisted of a dirt driveway and an unattended security gate. It didn't look like a place I should have been without an appointment. I parked just inside the gate, stepped out of my car and looked around for an employee.

There were cabins on the property, which looked like temporary housing for the fieldworkers. Around the corner of one came a brawny security guard.

"Yo quiro trabaca. Los fraises?" I called.

"Hah, you pick strawberries?" he replied as he approached.

"Yes, I heard you're hiring."

"Gringo, not here!"

On the other side of the street were nearly two hundred workers bending over in the fields, picking strawberries. *Not here, huh?*

The guard abruptly escorted me off the property. As I drove off, I experienced a good dose of culture shock.

I had been discriminated against!

The next day, I was driving along the fragrant fields of Gilroy, California, the Garlic Capital, only about forty-five minutes from where I grew up.

I had never been curious about the labor in the fields as a kid, but now I realized I didn't know much about the process or of the people that worked them. I drove back and forth along rows of farms, wondering how to contact someone in charge. I needed an opportunity to work in the fields, but I had little experience picking. I couldn't tell which sections of row crops were growing garlic, pepper, broccoli, artichoke or anything else.

I waited for a white pickup truck to drive from the center of the fields back to the main road, hoping to catch him. The only way I could make this happen, was to get straight to the point. I approached a businesslike Asian man and his field manager, whose name turned out to be Jorge.

"Can I have a job?"

"We start at five a.m.," he replied, looking me up and down doubtfully.

"That's fine by me."

He seemed to reconsider.

"Do you have papers?"

"Yes."

"Okay, I'll bring you employment forms. We pay $7.25/hr."

What a relief! After yesterday's fiasco, I had begun to lose hope of succeeding. Jorge handed me the hiring paperwork, every line of it in Spanish. I just signed next the 'x', grateful for the position, just as I imagined all my future co-workers felt. I was to report to Jorge early the next morning.

I couldn't find the right field in the early morning darkness. I noticed a man biking with reflectors and I followed. Loads of vans and personal cars sat on the road's shoulder with workers trying to get their last minutes of rest. Five a.m. struck and the lights of the tractor shone bright onto the fields of green peppers, ready to be picked.

I didn't remember Jorge's face well, as I was scrabbling around looking for my only contact, my new boss. Portapotty doors slammed, and people started filtering into their positions in the rows. One guy pointed toward my spot, where I was assigned. He must have known that I didn't speak Spanish because he just pointed. The sound of the tractor was deafening, not exactly the noise you want to hear first thing. I had to speak loudly, to be heard over the tractor.

"Donde esta Jorge?"

My boss wasn't there, so I went to my position and was handed a bucket. I glanced at what others were doing. I took a more detailed look, as I was stunned that they were picking green peppers so fast without pulling the plant from its roots.

One of the workers called me over to his plant and showed me not to harvest peppers that are too small, have reddish or brown color. I couldn't believe not only did I have to pick peppers at such a pace, but also carefully observe what I'm picking. He showed me how to lift the bush from underneath with one hand, to find the peppers that were hiding and to twist, not pull, the peppers off with the other hand.

I began to fill my bucket—thirty peppers, then walk them over to the conveyor belt, where the tractor would sort them and provide the package crew their duties. If I were to guess, my pace was a third my coworker's, but I did have a height disadvantage, meaning I was too tall. I found myself sitting on the rim of the bucket to give my back a rest. As the hours wore on, I snuck a seat more often and sat longer. I couldn't ask how long we had to do this because of my lack of Spanish, but we did seem to be running out of field, as the rows became overcrowded.

*Trying to keep pace with my fellow co-workers, as I try to fill
the bucket with green peppers outside of Gilroy, California*

Finally, the tractor shut off, and workers started piling into
white vans. I didn't know what we were expected to do next.
I followed in my Jeep, intuitively thinking we were headed to
another field for a new assignment.

That night, I decided not to go back to my parent's home to
sleep; they were tired of seeing me. They've never completely
understood the things that I do. And, they have every right to
make me feel uncomfortable if I rely on their support through
these, as they would say, waste of time endeavors.

So, I slept in my car just five miles from their house, in a
familiar neighborhood. It was lonely. Another sleepless night
contemplating my life and my unconventional path, while
knowing how lost they thought I was in life. They didn't know
why I needed to make life harder than it needed to be. So,
they didn't support me. I couldn't seem to gain approval from
anyone around me, no matter how often I proved that my
work was valuable on a personal and communal level.

Why did I put myself through this? Was it just curiosity? Was I trying to avoid the realities of real work or the work that is socially acceptable for a college graduate? Was I escaping from something? No, I wasn't.

I felt connected with the world through these humble experiences. I enjoyed the challenge. I enjoyed the variety of life. I was genuinely interested in the lives of others. That's why I was here, doing something that I didn't necessarily need to do. That's what my parents didn't understand.

As the sun came out that morning in the pepper fields, I was so glad to be in cooler temperature this week in Gilroy. The previous two weeks, I was in Bakersfield, located in Kern County of California's Central Valley. During my stint there, I baked in 116 degrees, fully clothed to protect myself from the blazing sun and the hazardous pesticides. I remember showing up to my first day of work at Murray Family Farms and noticed all my soon to be co-workers in clothing, no different than dressing for a harsh winter. I had learned how critical it was to cover every inch of skin. It wasn't common to see fieldworkers use sunscreen or sunglasses for that matter. The smog did provide a thick layer of protection from the sunrays although very hazardous. You couldn't even tell there was an enormous mountain range on the horizon.

Finding work in Kern County, one of the highest concentrations of undocumented immigrants, put me on the verge of wanting to give up. I stopped in a lobby of a hotel to refuge from the smoldering heat. As I was sitting contemplating a strategy, I got up to approach the front desk.

"Are you from here, Bakersfield?"

"Yes."

"Do you know any farms in the area where I can work?"

I didn't know where to begin. I didn't know the process of being hired and I didn't think I could just show up at a random field and ask to work.

"Take Highway 99, and drive to any gas station. You'll find many day laborers waiting to be picked up before 4:30 a.m."

I took Highway 99 to arrive here, and remembered seeing a hundred miles of fields, of all sorts. Afterall, California is the number one grower of most produce. In some fields I saw large silver tents lined up at the end of each row, where produce would be packaged right on the spot and delivered to the stores. In others, I saw huge crates stacked up in the middle of the fields, ready to be trucked to the stores. Step into a grocery store in Central California, and you'll find a wide variety of colorful produce piled halfway to the ceiling.

"You might want to dress in disguise, as you will stick out like a sore thumb, and show up at the corner gas station before 4:30am.," she continued. "They all have papers. I know people and they all have papers."

She acted defensive. I didn't care. I wasn't an undercover immigration officer, yet I imagine that's what many may have assumed as an American-born, English speaking job seeker. During my *50 Jobs in 50 States* journey, one of my jobs was working border patrol on the busy Mexico-Arizona border. I've seen what migrants go through to get here, whether wriggling through the sewers, burrowing tunnels or coming through the ports of entry with temporary visas to never return. I wanted to learn what they were coming for.

Growing up, whenever my father needed help on the yard, he'd drive to Home Depot parking lot, ask for a few eager workers and offer them an hourly wage. They'd get in his car, work until the job was complete, and get dropped off. That's a common practice in California and that's exactly what I wanted to do; day labor, but in the field.

Many American-born don't do this work. The census is that the work is too tough, and the pay is not high enough and there are no benefits. The employers are the beneficiary, and so are the consumers, if they don't have to cover insurance or provide a decent living wage for their workers. It's obvious that the undereducated and unskilled were being taken advantage of. There stood a sign, "Need immigration help? Get green cards and work permits fast. Buy immigration forms here!" This was obviously a scam.

After leaving the hotel lobby, I stopped by the United Farm Workers headquarters, a labor union that protects the rights of farm workers and asked for some advice and maybe a connection to land a job.

"They're not going to hire you. Many of the workers, let alone the employers, fear being exposed," a Latina female union representative assured.

"So, if I wanted a job, not as a journalist or for research, they wouldn't hire me?"

Coincidentally, she suggested approaching this the same way the hotel front desk did.

"If you show up at a corner store or gas station, you'd have to dress like the laborers, and hope to be selected. If you don't get picked, the laborers know the next spot to try."

She mentioned that her union tried a campaign, called Take Our Jobs. It was created to bring awareness to a common argument, that Mexicans and Central Americans are taking jobs away from American citizens. It allowed Americans to step into the shoes of a migrant fieldworker for a day. "Nobody has lasted more than a few hours," she said.

Her skepticism made me want to try this more than before. Nothing fuels me more than a challenge, although she was right. I wouldn't do this long-term. Even for the short-term, the oppressive heat put some doubt in my mind, as I was sweating just sitting in my car. Here I am, early August in an unassimilated community, not a word of English on any store fronts, billboards, street names. If I hadn't driven in, I would've mistaken it for a foreign country.

I looked for a spot to park and sleep for the night, ready to attempt this shot in the dark, gas station selection approach. Laying in my sweat, I felt I was already laboring before the next day began. I decided that for the remainder of the project, I was going to find a motel. I had to cut costs, wherever I could, but I realized I wasn't thinking clearly. A sleepless night filled with discomfort and anxiety made me groggy and unmotivated. I never made it to the gas station.

I didn't have the guts to show up at a gas station. If something went wrong, I'd be vulnerable, especially since there'd be a language barrier. I knew unions couldn't help me because they won't be able to hide what I shouldn't be seeing. I saw a billboard for Murray Family Farms right on the Highway 99. I called them before driving 60 miles to their location and got into questions that I was so curious about. I got a hold of Steve, the Human Resource Director. I told him that I'm looking for temporary work with migrant fieldworkers, just to understand the conditions of the industry. I could sense that he was very open and welcomed my employment.

"Are your workers documented?" I asked.

"Yes, but not having papers ain't no thing anymore," Steve stated.

"What do you think about the culture of people living under the radar?"

"It's insane. They are getting more and more comfortable about being illegal. We've been way too accommodating. They don't respect America. They burn our flag. We are forced to learn their language. They have no reason to assimilate. This doesn't happen in other countries."

Steve was frustrated to say the least. His farm only hires documented workers, but he admitted it's all fraudulent. He can't turn down an applicant if he has the paperwork, even though it's clearly fabricated. Verifying identification and background checks are too timely and costly. Plus, he needs people, and maybe that's why he was so quick to hire me.

Steve mentioned he's originally from Washington State and worked on a farm. He did that intense labor and mentioned that White people can do the work, but it's a political ploy. "It's just a way for employers to hire cheap labor and maximize profits," he said. Another reason Steve might have hired me over the phone was to prove that they'd hire anyone willing to work, no matter the background.

I was prepared for the morning to start at five a.m. and it felt like I was about to meet a group of the unknown world. Steve met me at the front of his retail shop, where many tourists visit. He introduced me to Octavio, who was a field leader and I was dropped off at a large orchard of apples. Rows and rows of apple trees, as far as you could see. Long black hoses that watered the crop, needed to be taken out from the ground and moved one row over.

I bent down, picked up the hose simultaneously with a team of four fieldworkers. We pulled it from the stubborn weeds that had grown over it, shook it to straighten the line and carried it five feet and laid it down.

We continued the monotonous move for the next three hours, covering forty plus rows. They continued a consistent pace, but I was slowing.

"This is what they're saying about back breaking work," I thought.

My co-fieldworkers couldn't see me from the distance, and I never responded to their calling out to me. They must have assumed I was a new Spanish speaking hire. I heard a bunch of singing and laughing, an unusual mood to be in for this type of work.

I found a long stick, sturdy enough to use as a tool. I didn't have time to refine it, but it helped me pick up the hose without bending and lift it to a more comfortable height, but my co-workers noticed I was slowing. This back breaking work could've been prevented by providing or innovating tools, but that's not the employer's priority.

I met with my new co-workers at lunch. The cafeteria table was a dirt floor parked with water coolers. They sat in a circle, eating homemade food. The only thing I recognized were tacos wrapped in tinfoil. I tried snapping a picture, but I didn't want them to assume I'm an investigator. Realizing that I didn't speak Spanish, they were telling lots of jokes in front of me...about me. I could feel some awkwardness, as I was standing outside the circle without anything to eat. One guy offered me something, but I refused because I didn't feel right about taking anything.

Lunchbreak with my new co-workers at Murray Family Farms in Bakersfield, California

All the guys wore large circled rim hats, jeans, thick flannel, and a piece of cloth laying over the neck. In this weather, I would've thought to wear shorts and a light t-shirt. The last thing I wanted to do was to overdress. Luckily, I packed a long sleeve shirt, jogging pants, and a hat. I learned that one of my co-workers was in his sixties. That gave me some comfort, for now. I thought, "if he could do it, I could do it."

We went back to the orchards and found a few more acres of rows to work relocating the hose. Around noon, the temperature had climbed above 116 degrees. The air was still. I wasn't prepared. No lunch. Improper clothing. I got a headache and the pollution caused my eyes to burn. I had to keep working through the headache because I didn't want to embarrass myself as a wimpy 'Gringo'. I was scheduled to work for two weeks with this crew.

Finally, we were allowed some rest time in the shade of the orchard. Remarkably, I heard multiple workers singing loudly and lots of laughter. Many of them making animal noises. Hearing the joy of them work, made me curious about their perspective and journey to get here. It seemed like a modern-day *Grapes of Wrath*, the John Steinbeck novel chronicling a journey of migration for work during the Great Depression.

Again, I imagined they were laughing about the new guy in the orchards.

"Tu es content?" my co-worker asks.

"No content." I replied.

"What excitement do you find doing this work?" I asked.

"Finishing!"

They were curious why I was working with them. Octavia mentioned to the crew I was writing a book to experience fieldwork and learn everyone's migration story. The stories were all too similar. Each one of them finding better work and opportunity than in their homeland, and to earn and send money back home to their family. I recalled what Steve mentioned, "they're opportunists, looking for easier work with higher pay, even if that means leaving their home."

We crawled into the back of a van and headed to the peach and fig trees. I was given a twelve-foot ladder and a large white bin with a strap to wrap around my neck. We each took a row of trees to harvest. The bin could hold up to fifty peaches, getting heavier and heavier with each pick. The climb on the ladder was more unstable. Lots of fruit was dropping from the tree. We were instructed to pick only store quality; ones with no blemishes or deformity. More than half the fruit went to waste. I felt guilty having to throw so much edible food to the ground. I would hope that a non-profit organization would gather the discarded fruit and process it for something beneficial. Still, I tried taking a bite into as many peaches and figs as I could, so at least I knew it wasn't wasted.

Packaging peaches, trying to overcome our language barrier.

The closest worker to my row, I spotted running up the ladder and filling his bin within minutes. That was the sixty-year-old.

"If they're getting hourly wage, why are they working so fast?" I thought. "Maybe that's their work ethic." Although, I started to move more swiftly on the ladder, there was no way that I was going to attempt the pace of my co-workers. It seemed they had a different level of drive.

My co-worker observed me watching him in awe. I called him Speedy Gonzales because that's the only thing I thought we'd mutually understand. He motioned with his hand, writing down something on paper, as if this was something worth noting for my book. I can tell he was being sarcastic.

Their sense of humor was contagious. The laughter and joyfulness kept the days short. I've never come across such cheerful workers, and this was the most difficult of conditions. It's no secret this is arduous work, but what came next was the most difficult assignment I've had in my life; pruning raspberry bushes. Given clippers, gloves, and a face mask, I dove into their thorny bushes nestled by barbed-wire. When I started clipping, dust like smoke bombs exploded off the vines and I occasionally spotted dead snakes and other rodents. The vines were feisty and stubborn. It was like playing tug of war with them. I noticed the singing and laughing subsiding, as this was a moment, I realized my co-workers were human after all.

*Toughest task was pruning raspberry
bushes in 116 degree temperatures*

I couldn't wait for the day to be over. And, that's the thing. You never know when the day will be over. We'd show up consistently in the morning, but the day could've been short or long, depending on the assignment. The day that I left at three o'clock was a good day.

I had time to drive to Cesar Chavez's grave, an American labor leader, community organizer, Latino American civil rights activist, and founder of the United Farmer Workers union. His tombstone read:

It's my deepest belief that only by giving our lives do we find life

Reflecting on my trek here, Cesar's statement answered my question of why I am doing this. I didn't change these people's lives, but I felt I was truly living by recognizing and appreciating the lives of others. Maybe my co-workers cherished that I was getting to know them, when they understood that I didn't need to.

"You must be rich, if you're going home tomorrow! You don't need job?" one fieldworker asked jokingly. One thing for sure, we all made new connections with a world outside our own.

Back in Gilroy, sitting in a folding chair on the shoulder of the road, I purchased a freshly made Mexican meal, prepared by a woman with her kids in tow. I sipped on my aloe water, chatting with my co-workers under an umbrella after tilling the soil of broccoli fields.

*Just completed manicuring a broccoli field and
wasn't sure where we were headed next*

"How long have you been here?"

"Sixteen years."

"Where do you live?"

"In an apartment with my wife and five kids. They're in school right now."

He continued, "I had to sneak two of them in."

Coming into America, whether legally or not, is not cheap. From my border patrol experience, I knew immigrants were willing to pay between \$500–\$20,000 to get across the border. My compassion grew, as I stepped into the daily lives of immigrants trying to make a better life. These people are unseen and unheard, but they're right off the highway in groups harvesting what you eat.

Missionary in Appalachia

*A*fter nine hours of driving, I'm lost. My cell phone is out of reception. My GPS brought me in circles, and the mountains didn't allow me to see passed an 1/8 of a mile. There is no landscape in the United States quite like the Appalachia Region. The environment secludes itself from the outside world, as it's hard to get in and hard to get out.

I had left my fiancé behind in Washington DC where she lives and works a full-time job as a paralegal. She had no interest in coming along with me to serve as a missionary in America's poorest county.

"Don't go," she expressed.

"I know, I don't want to. Trust me. I don't want to go back to Appalachia," I replied.

A few years ago, I worked as a coal miner in West Virginia. It was an experience that greatly helped me appreciate the hard work, sacrifice, and commitment people make for themselves, family, and the community. Putting myself in precarious situations, while working 4 miles underground, I never wanted to experience the work again, yet, I was still curious enough to understand how people live in extreme poverty and what are the real social issues that keep the region from prospering.

I never felt safe in Appalachia. Or should I say uncomfortable or out of my element? The weather is unpredictable, the roads are narrow and unmarked, and the towns are mostly unincorporated.

I was on my way to Appalachia Reach Out, a Christian-based missionary that serves the needs of the local community. The community that I was hoping to reach was Inez, located in Martin County, where World News Tonight featured a story. Diane Sawyer's episode covered the issues of drug abuse, rotting teeth, and the lack of education. Nothing good.

When reaching out to several mission programs across Appalachia, from Tennessee to Pennsylvania, I was only offered to help restore homes. Many students and other youth groups spend summer months repairing people's homes, listed as hazardous living conditions. I opted out of that type of service because I wanted to get to know the people of the region and understand their day-to-day lives, a way to make a social change.

Will Ruthigen, Director of Appalachia Reach Out was honored to accept my assistance. After all, I had planned my visit during off-peak missionary months, and he needed help.

"You're more than welcome to come work with me. I'm very blessed you have found us," Will explained. He researched my work experiences across America, after I explained that I would love to be involved first-hand with the community in ways that would be impactful.

"I think your message would speak hope and a bright future in lives of students that we often visit at the county high school."

He spoke in a very calm and soothing tone that seemed too pleasant to be genuine.

In order to find my way slowly to his campus, I parked my car incidentally in someone's driveway, the only place to pull over for miles.

Slowly walking towards me was a lady from her screen door.

"I'm looking for Pheasant Road. Do you know where I can find it?" I asked.

"Which way you coming from?" she laughs.

I suspected many people get lost in her driveway. Her next-door neighbor looked like was having a 24-7 yard sale, with clothes draped over the fence and miscellaneous items on the lawn. This was common, as residents try to earn money however they can.

"I'm trying to find Appalachia Reach Out," I replied.

"Oh you've got to head towards town and once you see the grocery store, bear left over the creek."

Her direction may have been clear to her, but I just smiled and nodded until I was back in my car. I figured I would leave her property and find someone else in town.

Four miles later, I pulled into a school parking lot and walked into the back of the building. I was looking for anyone that was familiar with ARO. I spotted a young lady teaching a group of teenage kids.

"Excuse me, but do you guys know where I can find ARO?"

Once again, I was given vague directions. Finally, my cell phone service was restored, and I found the campus. It was tucked right in the mountain with a beautiful stream flowing through, but from what I've heard, rivers and streams in Appalachia are most likely tainted by coal runoff. In the parking lot was only large passenger vans and a basketball hoop. I ring the doorbell, only to meet Jan, Will's wife.

"You're Daniel, right?"

"Yes, I'm looking for Will."

"He's on an errand right now but let me bring you to your room."

We walked across the lot, over a bridge, and into a 160-bunk bed building. Looking around, I felt alone, knowing that the place is usually packed with joyous youth. Jan leaves me to get settled, and the pick of many beds.

"We usually charge, but Will mentioned that your service is much appreciated."

He had scheduled a jam-packed week of speaking to high school students about my journey of work, a way for them to learn life outside their county. Other plans included making home visits, hospitals, and working at the food bank.

That night, I walked back to the main house, where Will and Jan stay. It was another large multi-story building that was sectioned off for several families to live.

"Come on up," Will stated.

As I walked up stairs, the television was tuned on a baseball game. The television set was surrounded with family photos and framed quotes from Jesus.

"You've made it," Will said in his casual tone. He looked just as I pictured from his voice. He had a welcoming and friendly appearance, wearing a collared shirt with jeans and in his socks.

"Yeah, it wasn't easy. Man, we are in the middle of the mountains, aren't we?" I mentioned.

"Yep, all around us," he agreed.

Ever since, I left Maryland and the DC area, all I could see were mountains. The only opening that I noticed on my drive were shopping centers, where a mountain was blown to make room. Pro-coal billboards and blasting zone signs were common sightings. Other than that, roads are like winding streams that are lined with coal train tracks and neighborhoods shoved along the roads. Appalachia Reach Out's property was as grand as I saw that day. There were huge grass fields between the buildings that made the space open, like we were in a valley.

"Well, you ready for tomorrow? By the way, what is your faith?" Will asked.

We didn't have this conversation before my arrival, as he probably assumed everyone that serves his organization admits Jesus as their Lord and Savior.

"I tend to keep that personal," I responded.

I didn't want him to kick me out, if I didn't believe what he does.

"Aren't you scared about being in this area, with all the bad things going on around here?" I asked.

"My wife and I made the sacrifice to Jesus and were open to wherever our services are needed. We had moved from Grand Rapids, Michigan, where we left a lot of family behind for eight years. To answer your question, I don't fear anything. I have submitted myself to Jesus and accept whatever he chooses," Will stated.

If you could take fear out of the equation, life would be so much more stress-free. That night, in my empty building of a room, I was thinking about how vulnerable I was. No locks on the door, uncertain environment, no neighbors, howling wind, and dark, very pitch dark. I moved the dresser in front of the door, kept the lights off, even in time of need to detract any attention. I laid there, listening to the shuffling of nature.

The next morning, Jan and Will welcomed me to their kitchen table for breakfast. It was a pleasure being hosted by a health-conscious family, replacing syrup with agave to go with pancakes and fruit.

"Want a beverage?" Jan asked.

"I'll take water," I replied.

"Bottled water is our only option." Jan stated

Consuming tap water is asking for a sentence with cancer. As I later learned, water consumption is one of the lowest demanded fluids.

Will and I head to the county high school, where I was to make presentations to a few English classes. Standing in the entrance was Karen, the school's social service coordinator. This was a staff position that I wasn't familiar with in other areas of the country.

"We are so glad you've dedicated your time. What kind of message will you be sharing with our students today?" Karen asked.

"Life's what you make it. I hope to encourage students to open up their worlds, be curious and learn from others. To set goals in the classroom and in the real world, not to just go through the motions. It's important to apply and connect what we learn and recognize how it can benefit us," I stated.

"Perfect. Everyone is so excited to meet a celebrity. We've been watching your videos all of yesterday." Karen mentioned.

It was kind of cool, that people were familiar with my adventures being secluded in the mountains. As I was being introduced to a few kids passing through the hallways of a cooking class, I noticed they were chugging cans of Mountain Dew. I felt it was like I was meeting celebrities, hearing all about this soda habit, being right before my eyes. Through my research of the region, I heard that rotting teeth of teenagers was common because of the addiction to the soft drink.

"Wanna try my fried pancake that I made?" a kid asked. "Just be honest. How do you like it?"

I asked for a clean fork and stabbed a piece off his plate.

"Well, it's not that good," I replied.

"Hahahah, ohhhhh," his class responded.

"Let me ask you something. It's 7am, why are you drinking soda?" I inquired.

"It's gets you up and going. Plus, it's good," he replied.

I was ushered to the English class, where I would spend most of the day. I look around at the kids, not noticing a difference between them and other high school kids around the country. Just your ordinary kids, but what they go through is not. Plastered around the school halls are posters addressing starvation. One poster read:

"Just because you're in school, doesn't mean you're all there."

I was unaware of how many students are left home to starve, while being in school was their only chance to eat.

"Did you notice that pawn shop that we passed on the way to school?" Karen asked.

"Yes, Will pointed that out to me."

"Well, a majority of our community relies on welfare, including food stamps. Many parents use those food stamps to purchase Mountain Dew from the grocery store and resell it to the pawn shop for a higher value. Then they use that cash to feed their drug habit. Most likely, prescription drugs," Karen explained.

"Whaaaaat, that's insane. So, these kids actually don't have money to eat?" I asked concerned, thinking about this epidemic.

"Nope, we give them free lunch and snacks, so if you're interested in helping to pass out the snacks, let me know," Karen stated.

"Of course, where does the school get the money to feed all these kids?" I asked.

"Well, thankfully it's not every kid in school, but we do get support from the government and local donations," she replied. Karen seemed to have a career where she couldn't focus on herself. She's living in a community, constantly worrying about others.

At the break from classroom presentations, Karen invited Will and I to visit a lunchtime heritage festival held at the local elementary school. Interestingly enough, to make room for the massive school building, it looked like another mountain was blown. We walk on the long driveway, Karen having trouble breathing.

"I'm thirsty, I need to get a Diet Coke," she said aloud.

"That's not good for thirst," I suggested. It was a bit humid in early Fall, but it wasn't unseasonal in this part of the country.

"Do you drink water?" I asked curiously.

"No, never," Karen replied.

I turned to Will in awe. I didn't want to say much else, just continued walking up the driveway.

Laid out on six folding tables was a smorgasbord of local foods. We arrived late, so there wasn't much left besides the vegetables. There was a similar theme that I noticed at the high school. The veggies were in the trash. "You can lead a horse to water, but you can't make it drink," I thought about the government's push towards healthy foods.

"We're still barbequing, so you won't be left hungry," a lady mentioned, wearing a shirt "Coal Blooded".

We walk over to the gun demonstration on the side of the yard, where the instructor was sharing with elementary kids how he built his gun and what it takes to load.

"Why don't you let our guest from California try," Karen asked.

"Noooo, no no. I'm good," I responded.

I didn't want to come all the way to Appalachia and get myself hurt. Heck, the gun was homemade. Sure, enough, out of peer pressure from the young crowd, I gave it a whirl. And, sure enough, the ammunition got stuck and blew out smoke.

"I'm done." I assertively said.

"No, no. I've got it fixed," the instructor insisted.

I couldn't believe this scene, where I was in the middle of Eastern Kentucky, at an elementary school with students observing a novice gun shooter, while Christian music was being blasted throughout the festival.

"Alright, fine," I said. I put the rifle against my shoulder, move my face far from the gun and closed my eyes to shoot and hit the lamp post against the mountain. It wasn't fun, but just a part of the motions.

Man shows off his homemade gun to kids at a local elementary school in Inez, Kentuck

We went back to the high school, where I finished with three other classes and then handed out snacks to the underprivileged students. If you're wondering what kinds of foods were dished out, it was chips and soda or high sugared fruit drinks.

"Want to come chew with us after school," a student asked.

"No, I'm good." I responded.

I could tell, he asked me to test if I was manly enough to handle tobacco. He wanted to show me that people are rough out here. In the following days, I would get to see how rough people were.

Will and I headed back to ARO's campus, where I was getting ready for another sleepless night. I wanted to ask Will if he had another place to sleep that was closer to the main house, but I didn't want to have him ask why.

The following morning, we left early to make home visits. This is where Will shares his spirit of religion with the elderly and sick. Typically, unannounced, we ventured home to home. He would honk his horn driving by homes of people he knew, just to let them know that he's thinking about them. I was looking forward to this day because it would give me a chance to learn about the locals and their needs. We drove way off the main road, into, what you would call a "hollow." The locals say "holler." The roads are very narrow, mostly unmarked, that are surrounded by mountains on both sides and a creek between. There's only one-way in and the same way out. Mostly, these hollows are claimed through generations by families.

"Can I help you guys with something?" an alert man asked. He was like a pit-bull. It was obvious he wanted us out of his hollow.

"We're headed up to see Janice," Will said.

We continued up the windy dirt road walled by thick shrubs and pine trees. We spot Janice's yard from a distance, but are only able to make the rest of the way on foot. A few dogs, looked to be tied, are barking like wild. I opted to go back to the car, but Will asked for me to be fearless.

"Don't worry, just ignore them," he said.

Miraculously, we made it passed the dogs and into the backdoor of Janice's home. Her place was all wood, from floor to roof. It looked like a good storm would crush it.

"Come on in Will. Who's your guest?" Janice asked.

Janice was an elderly lady that anticipated visits from Will once a week. She was living alone, unable to drive, and needed attention. I was a bit uneasy walking in. A duck just walked out of her kitchen, as I couldn't tell where the outside of the home and inside started.

Why don't you come in son?" Janice requested.

I walked cautiously, trying not to touch anything with my bare skin, as I was also trying to hold my breath. Looking above her kitchen table, I see a tape hanging from the ceiling to catch insects. Her stove was wood-fire, bathroom was like an outhouse, and the gas heater was lit.

"Sit down Daniel," Will asked.

I didn't want to sit, I just wanted to go back outside, but then again there were those dogs. Will could tell I wanted to leave, so he gave me his car keys, where I waited in the car.

"Gosh, I'm such a wuss!" I thought to myself. "I came here to make a difference and I knew I would be out of my element, so what's up with me?" Not having health insurance, made the risks even higher.

After a half an hour contemplating all the varied challenges across the country that I faced, Will existed ready to leave. I felt I was being rude by just walking out and sitting in the car. I'm sure Will concocted an excuse for my absence.

"Why don't you sit on that tire swing, that's a real hillbilly thing to do," Will suggested.

I snapped a photo sitting in the tire with the creek view behind me. I wasn't feeling good about myself, posing for a picture with no substance behind it. As we headed to the next home, I was trying to build up courage to stay for the entire visit. All I had to do was visit. Just be company.

"We're going to meet with another elderly lady, but she is very ill. She has cancer from the pollutants in the water," Will prepared me. We stopped by her next-door neighbor to make sure our visit time was orderly.

"Yes, she's been expecting you," the neighbor claimed.

In her home were smoke intoxicated walls and ceilings. "Come on Daniel, do it for the book you're writing?" Will encouraged.

I walked into her kitchen, where she offered us noodle soup with chicken meatballs. As I watched her pour our bowls, I noticed her cancerous arm. Her arm was triple the size of her other one. After she set our bowls on the table and asked us to take a seat, I was once again trying to slowly move towards the exit door. I couldn't bear to stand there infused with cigarette smoke.

"Daniel, we'll only be a minute. Sit down and have some soup," Will insisted.

I sat down, trying to overcome discomfort that I felt during the first visit. "You can do this," I thought. As we were sipping our soup, she rolled up her sleeve and showed me her arm.

"Look how it's spreading," she said. She did something that made me just want to walk out. She twisted her arm, having it bend in an unusual motion.

"I have to take this phone call, I'll be back." I pulled the phone from my pocket.

"But you didn't finish your soup." She glanced at the full bowl.

Once again, I waited by the car. "This is more difficult than I expected it would be," I thought. Will returned to meet me, after having his lunch. "Do you think you could come to another house with me today?" Will asked.

"I don't know. Is there anything else I could do?" I was admiring Will's courage and dedication.

"Just come to one more with me. This lady is healthy and lives in a nice place, she just needs a prayer for her lost husband."

We drove to Edna's home, which was situated in the prairie on the base of the Appalachian Mountain. Her living room contained a coal fired boiler. In her yard was the family cemetery, which was common in this part of the country. Her husband was just buried a few months earlier.

"Will, pray for me. I know I'm next," Edna stated.

Will said a few words and then asked about how things were going.

"Oh, just trying to survive. Have you talked with Aldine today?" she asked.

"It's been a few weeks."

Edna dialed Aldine for Will to speak with. It seemed like an urgent matter.

"Aldine had a seizure last night that left a huge gash on her forehead. She's having some family drama over yonder," Edna whispered as the phone was ringing.

"I'll be right over Aldine, I'm going to bring a visitor with me," Will said.

After an hour drive through the windy hills, we approach a cluster of homes, modest in size. The one that didn't have a driveway, was Aldine's.

"Come on in Brother Will, where's your friend?" she asked.

I was hesitant of going inside, but had to finish the day off with at least one visitation. This is what I've asked for; to get to know the people of Appalachia, but I find myself unadaptable.

"Come on in, Daniel," she invited. "I'm not ashamed of what I got."

I had to go in now, especially if it made her feel comforted. She offered us some local cookies and tea, but I was content with not having any. I didn't want to prolong the visit.

We sat her on colonial style furniture, where her living room was decorated with Jesus portraits, family photos, and classic artwork. I sat in the distance of the room, observing my surrounding. She got up and offered to give us a tour. First, she showed us the scene, where she collapsed on the bathroom floor, leaving her with a swollen forehead. She explained that she was flat on the floor, trying to aid herself. She didn't have anyone to help, having been disconnected from her family.

Listening to Edna's story of how she fell and
hit her head from a recent seizure

"How come they don't love me, Brother Will?"

"There's nothing you can do, but keep believing in God and the people that he brings in and out of your life," Will stated in a calming tone. You can sense his expertise delivering advice.

"Would they accept me if I wore a blonde wig when I went out?" she continued.

I didn't comprehend the situation that she was in. Will later explained to me that she's a very traditional Appalachian woman who still wears the bonnet, long dresses, and is a strong follower of evangelical Christianity. Her immediate family doesn't approve of her lifestyle, as they are ashamed of her beliefs.

Interestingly enough, I didn't believe that was the case for the excommunication. It had to be something else.

"Is it because of the money?" Aldine cried. She sat in her chair sobbing.

"What money?" I asked.

"When my parents both passed, I was given the entire hillside of coal. I was the only one in the family to take care of my sick parents," she explained.

"I'd love you for 5 acres of coal," I said jokingly to break the sobbing mood.

"Hahaha, he's cute ain't he?" Aldine said to Will.

Aldine's next door neighbors were her family. She hadn't spoken to them in almost six years. As I look at Aldine sitting in her chair weeping, behind her through the window was the home of her brother. Will and I both left, leaving Aldine feeling comforted by our presence.

"Just having us visit and listen is healing and will make her day," Will stated as we walked to his car.

We headed back to the campus, where I started to feel comfortable, sort of a safe haven from the surrounding areas. We both were ready to eat dinner that his wife prepared. With Jan was one of ARO's helpers, Ester. She's a native of the area and explained to me, that she comes from one of the hollows nearby. "I got married at 14, to the only boy my age in the hollow. He was my love," she stated.

Ester's love died in a coal mining accident, which was common in the 1950's. She reflected on her poor childhood, where she was walking to school shoeless and had to focus on working rather than school. Now in her late 50's, she looked twenty years older.

Will invited over his friend and colleague, Dallas, who was a former coal miner.

"Yep, I shoveled coal for 26 years, now I have black lung and a missing finger."

Disability was common in the Appalachia area. Thirty-six percent of the Martin County population is registered as disabled. Not only because of the coal industry.

"Some are legitimate injuries that depend on government assistance, but many are not. There are not many people checking on the status," Dallas continued. It was clear that he was an honest, hardworking man. He couldn't comprehend the motto *working to live,* he only understood *living to work.*

Both guests start singing, sharing a song with me after our meal. "This old hollow....."

It sounded like a foreign language, although it was clearly their Appalachian dialect.

Ester's story is familiar in Eastern Kentucky, as when Dallas explained his background, it was like déjà-vu. He had quit school at the age of fourteen to start working, in order to support his family.

After the dinner, the guests leave, while Will and I were scheduled to watch Shelby High's girls' soccer game

"I'm going to take out the trash honey, then me and Daniel are going to the field," Will said.

I headed out with Will to help carry the loads of waste. We went down a slope by the creek, where I saw residue from a fire pit. I learned that was their recycling program. Set it on fire. I wondered why I was seeing so many small fires throughout the night when we drove around town.

Will piles his recycling before setting it on fire

On an unseasonably cold night, Will and I arrived at the field, where I had previously met a few of the players during my presentations. Not too many people in the stands, so we decided to sit in the car and watch the game from the window shield. Big as the scoreboard, a billboard of the 10 Commandments.

"That's very unusual, Will. Isn't this a public school?" I asked. I shouldn't have been surprised, knowing that 5 of the 6 radio stations in town were Christian.

"Yes, but the funding for the field and much of the school and the City of Inez comes from the coal operator. He wanted the billboard if he agreed to constructing this field. Remember that home that I showed you? That's his."

It was a home large as the White House, sticking out like a sore thumb amongst the rest of the community. As we continue to watch the game, the coach was getting into one of his athlete's face.

"You're only good for staying home and making babies," he blurted out.

She starts to cry, as we noticed her mother pulling up in her car beside us. Her daughter ran over to explain what had just happened. The mom gets out of the car, wearing a leather jacket with a cigarette in her mouth.

"What are you saying to my daughter?" the mom yells. The coach walks over in the middle of play and they start arguing.

Things just didn't seem right in Inez. Looked like there was drama anywhere you went. At this point, I started to see how Will and his missionary program were a much-needed service to fight the Devil, as he had put it.

We headed back to the campus, where we saw a group of teenagers on the side of the road, decorating a memorial for a lost classmate; a sight too frequent for how precious life is.

I would spend a few more nights before departing to the region's most impoverished county, Owsley. The following days, I went with Will and Dallas to make hospital visits to make any last prayers requested by patients. I stood in the hallway shielding my discomfort of going into the room by the compliance of health, safety and privacy regulations of the patients.

Will and Jan suggested I spend the weekend with them because they were planning a visit to a festival called, Apple Days. Heritage festivals, especially in the summer are popular in the mountain regions. I was about to experience a lot of culture and history. When we arrived, the authenticity of the people showed. Thousands of guests shared a weekend playing local games, artwork, tapestry, listening to bluegrass music, and preachers. It was worth staying throughout the weekend because it was interesting to see life as it was. Not an ounce of outside influence, from the fact that very few people carried cell phones, one hundred percent of the crowd was white, mostly Scotch-Irish. Hip-hop didn't seem to influence the youth, as it does in most communities. People were what they were; working class, coal mining, mountain men and women, and most importantly unfettered.

Local festival of the Appalachia Region

Leaving the festival in an old Cadillac Deville was a large group of burly men, with thick beards and trucker hats. Their weight dragged down the vehicle as it was crawling up the mountainous highway. It was captured by the sight unique to this region of America.

Early next morning, I left Inez and my new friends, Will and Jan, for a trip to Daniel Boone National Forest. It was a beautiful drive, with stunning scenery, which made it hard to imagine that I was headed for the poorest county in the Appalachia region. Typically, major cities, like Chicago or Atlanta, segregate wealthy and poor, but Kentucky as a state, clearly has the same features. Horse country, near Lexington and Louisville has strong industries, whereas on the Eastern side of the National Forest, you have the Appalachia region, which for centuries has been depressed.

Owsley County sits right on the National Forest boundary. As I approach the welcome sign, I stopped to the take a picture.

Within seconds, an angry dog barked to my welcoming. I jumped back into my car, double checked the distance to my destination, and took a deep breath. I had agreed to work with another service group, but my contact had been unclear of my tasks or where I could be accommodated for a week.

"I'll meet you tomorrow. Just get checked into your room," Sheena stated.

Three weeks ago, when I made some desperate calls to find a willing service group to volunteer, Sheena, the non-profit's director had me connect with the local thrift store, where I was offered to sleep on the store's floor. I declined the offer, after they mentioned they inadvertently had a sexual predator stay there.

I followed my notes of directions, observing the town's environment. As I crossed over a bridge, I felt something was very eerie about this town, called Booneville. I approach this rotary, which circles around a courthouse. Across the street from the historic building were boarded up windows, only showing brick and wood. On a weekday during the afternoon, not a soul in sight. I circled the entire structure, which could've led me right back out of town or down a slight hill into a shopping center. I use the term, shopping center, loosely. There was only the thrift shop, which offered a place for me to stay, which was closed and Family Dollar. I figured I'd get a snack from the store, not knowing if I'd get another chance. I walked in, people staring at me. Just staring at me. I walked in and walked right back out. Although, that couldn't have drawn more attention.

I got back into my car, decided to check into my room, not knowing what kind of place it was at all. I scouted the town as I was looking for my destination and noticed a vacant factory, where two people make some kind of sketchy exchange, which couldn't be good. I turned around, when I realized I passed my place. I parked my car, walked out, look around. I didn't feel good. I felt lonely. I felt out of place. I wondered what I was doing in Booneville.

I look for someone to ask if I was in the right area. I approach this lady, looking at old thrifty clothing.

"Excuse me, is this the church where people stay?"

She didn't bother turning around. She ignored me. I felt like going back to Inez.

I hear yelling. Vicious yelling. Those that were looking at the thrift sale turned around. I turned around.

Across the street was a gas station. I see a guy escaping a headlock; his white t-shirt had just been torn. I inch closer, as those around stood still. It was a brawl.

A large bearded man opened his driver's door and took out his axe, as his accomplice gets the guy with the ripped shirt in another headlock. The bearded man started to swing, trying to behead this guy. Ten to fifteen people are involved; more axes come out, big trucks block the way. Bystanders observe from the sidelines. I was about to witness a murder.

I didn't know what to do. Should I help, should I get back in my car? I opted for the latter. I got back in my car, started the engine, all while trying to see what was going on.

"Call the sheriff," is what I heard from my slightly opened window. When I see a man jump on to another person's moving truck, that's when I was out of there.

I crossed back over the bridge, leading out of Booneville and never turned back. I saw the sheriff on his way to the scene, thinking he's going to get there way too late.

I was entering Beattyville, my next assignment, a week early, where I drove straight to the campus of Cumberland Mountain Outreach, directed by Cindy Feller. When I pull into her driveway, I spotted her mowing the hilly terrain of a lawn. She sees me, and lifts her arm up to waive, as she continued mowing.

I walked around her property, reflecting on my experiences from Booneville. I had wondered if I should bring it up, or maybe I would appear to be a sheltered adult.

"Hey, I wasn't expecting you until next week," Cindy says.

"I know, I just thought I'd come early. I have this rental car and I didn't want the costs to add up," I replied.

"Well, let me show you around and then you can get settled."

I was hoping she would have me stay in her house, which was also on the property, but she brought me to a two-bedroom cabin, surrounded with ten others the same size.

"It's chilly and it's gonna drop in the 30's tonight. Let me get you a space heater," Cindy said.

I looked around, and although it was relatively pleasant, I wanted to get back in my car and drive to Washington DC and forget the entire thing, but I did realize that just being a helping hand is a significant contribution. I went for a run around the neighborhood, just casually looking at the homes. I was on steep slope after slope. I noticed a police car in a driveway directly across from where I was staying, so I felt a bit more secure.

Unexpectedly, Cindy invited me out to dinner with her fiancé and neighbor. I hadn't noticed any restaurants around town, but we ended up eating at Dairy Queen, which is the only fast food chain in the county. As we were chatting at our table, I noticed a lady in her late twenties sobbing next to two of her kids.

"What is going on with this place?" I thought. I brought that to the attention of Cindy. She turned around, took a glance, and right back into our discussion. "What do you think she's crying about?"

"Her boyfriend or husband is probably in jail and she's taking care of the kids," she states. Cindy has been in the social services business for thirty years, so she was confident on her understanding of the situation. She's originally from Ohio and found passion in working with those in need, especially children.

When I went to pick up our order, I stopped by a table with four police officers. I noticed one of them didn't have teeth. I mentioned my brief experience in Booneville, watching a brawl. They weren't surprised.

"That's Booneville for ya!," an officer stated. I told them that I was from out of town, trying to understand the way of life in Owsley County.

"People are only here if they're dumb or lost," he suggested.

"What's up with the prescription drug abuse here?"

"Oh, it's bad. Just the other day, my dentist kept pushing me pills, even when I told them I don't want it. He was so persistent on giving me the drugs; I had to tell him that I'm a police officer."

"So, he's getting some kind of commission?"

"Yeah, that's how it works around here. In Booneville, there's no police force, so they must rely on a single sheriff, which is corrupt himself. He takes bribes and runs quite an operation over there."

"Thanks for the info guys," I said.

"Yeah, good luck on your mission," they responded.

I sat back down with my group, where I was informed more about the area. Beattyville used to be a boomtown for oil, and then the refinery just got too expensive to operate. There's not much coal in this part of the state, so people were living on three generations of poverty. Churches are going bankrupt because they are overextending their needs to provide for the community.

"We're going to take you to church with us tomorrow morning," Cindy suggested.

I hadn't experienced Appalachia until I visited the church. Located off the gravel road, a church from a trailer hosted hundreds of attendees. I sat down for an early Bible discussion with a smaller group, learning the meaning behind each verse. As I sat there, listening to those contributing, I couldn't help but to think how polarized communities like Beattyville, Booneville, and Inez are. I was sitting amongst good hearted people, living in peace, trying to strengthen themselves and those around them. On the contrary, the other half of the society was bringing the community down.

Just picture this. If you arbitrarily drop a group of individuals in the mountainous forest, like Appalachia, you will have half of the people believing in a high power and there's more to life than just what's seen, and then you'll have those that would take advantage and be destructive. That's what you have right here, in Owsley County.

Cindy introduced me to her daughter, son-in-law, and their two daughters. They were wonderful church-going people that moved from Florida to live for cheap. They offered to take me to breakfast and introduce me to the local dishes. As I was sipping my corn stew, the two daughters were talking about their pet goats. After breakfast, they wanted to show them to me.

We drove to their house, as we pulled up to the driveway; the father noticed something that didn't look right. The fenced door looked like it had been pushed open. He ran up to the goat's cage, put his hands in his face, and turned around. The kids, waiting in the car had a feeling something wasn't right. They looked on with concern from the backseat next to me.

"They're done. Completely slaughtered!" The dad's ruddy face was grim.

The girls started crying and I was offered a ride back to Cindy's home.

After a restless night of sleep, I got ready to work for the City of Beattyville's social service department, arranged by Cindy. I had a chance to volunteer at a food pantry, where I worked with local individuals to hand out food and other essentials to the elderly. I got to know a few of the volunteers and hear their stories. I've never heard anything like it.

"Yep, I'm born and raised right here. It's a rough place. We could easily set up this town for tourism because of the National Forest, but we don't want any outsiders," one lady explained.

She continued to tell me her family life.

"My brother was hanging out with his friends and then they just gutted him, right in front of me. They took out his heart and laid it on his chest."

"What!"

"People are crazy out here. A family of six was burned in their trailer in the middle of the night because there was a rival family. I'm sure you're familiar with the Hatfield-McCoy feud, well there's many families that have generational feuds."

After handing out food for the entire morning, I was given a tour of the county's back roads and just when you think there's a dead-end, the road keeps going. I'm thankful that I'm not from the area.

"There's some hollows that you don't ever want to go down. They'll kill anyone they don't know."

I was scheduled to work the following day, but I just left. That was enough.

I filled up my gas tank, waved to a cop. I'm frozen in thought, staring at him. We had a striking resemblance, not just esthetically.

"That's the Appalachia version of me," I thought.

This life could've been my own.

Gettin' Fit in Mississippi

$\mathcal{E}$very Sunday morning, Saddie MacDonald gets ready for church. She's pushing the age of seventy-two, but after staying with her for a few days, I would've guessed twenty years younger. As a librarian, caretaker of her diabetic husband, and the nucleus of her extended family, I couldn't believe she had the energy to take on anything more. But she did. So, when she asked me if I wanted to go to with her to the service, answering I was too tired wasn't an option.

Here I am in the Deep South in the middle of small-town Mississippi, about to attend a Southern Baptist Church, an uplifting and energetic experience I've only heard about. Saddie is the only church member that crosses the train tracks to the other side of town each Sunday. She lives in a white neighborhood, where a town still lives divided.

While Saddie was in her Sunday best, I on the other hand only packed athletic attire for my mission of training the most obese community in America for a 5k Turkey Trot road race. I managed to dress as formally as possible with what I brought.

Saddie told me that Rev. Ray Williams was expecting me at church that day.

"He's not gonna have me introduce myself, is he?" I asked.

"I bet he will," she said. "He wants to let people know what you're doing in town."

My heart skipped a beat at the thought of California-urbanite me explaining to a rural black community why I was in their church. I've never surrounded myself in this type of environment and it made me nervous. I wasn't sure what they'd think of me, or even if I'd be accepted. Regardless, I put myself in this situation and that's what I had to do.

When we reached the stairs of the largest member church in town, nobody was staring at me as I'd expected they would. Although I felt out of place, I didn't feel unwelcomed. I will admit my mind was feeding into being judged.

"Mornin', Mrs. MacDonald," a member welcomed Saddie.

I learned that everyone calls each other by mister or miss in the South. It's a respectful way of greeting or addressing one another.

"Good morning," she said. "I want you to meet Daniel. He's from California."

Her introduction got me a couple smiling hellos and handshakes before entering church. The sound of the all-male choir was welcoming, and the music of the organ and drums were soothing. I felt relaxed. While watching members dancing from the ground floor to the balconies, I realized my concerns about attracting attention were in vain.

"This is just a rehearsal, cuz when we get to Heaven, we're gonna really sing," the choir sang.

A little girl ran up and hugged me. I didn't recognize her at first, being in a fancy pink dress, hair in curls, and a touch of make-up. I'd met her and the mother two nights ago during the town hall meeting, that I advertised around town with posters and flyers.

On a dark and stormy night, in a rented community center, I stood in a large room, packed with folding chairs and a discouragingly small number of community members to fill them.

"Was I nuts for being here and trying to do this?" I thought.

I had already made the trip and spent months planning, I still had to give it my best effort. I assured myself I could do it as I stared into the eyes of the twelve curious audience members.

"Every excuse is a good excuse," I exclaimed after my burning question, "is 20-30 minutes of your day too much to ask for your health?"

I was listening to the statement of my own, a much-needed remedy for my anxieties. In fact, I could've blamed anything besides myself for the lack of participation I had already experienced that first night. There were a bunch of excuses up my sleeve ready to go since I expected a minimum of a hundred people in a tight-knitted community like Pickens, with a population of 1,200.

The path to Pickens was a test of my will. Just when I felt on my last straw before arriving, I did an online Google search for the mayor's office phone number, just to confirm my visit. There read: *Mayor of Pickens tragically dies in a car wreck.*

"But that can't be possible? I just spoke with him on the phone a few days ago," I thought.

My mind was spinning. I knew there was another town called Pickens, located in South Carolina, so this couldn't have been the mayor who I'd spoken to. I clicked on the link to the story, and my eyes widened with shock. I felt a chill going down my spine. I started getting teary, feeling remorse, thinking about his family and the rest of the town. This must be an absolute tragedy for such a small community. I didn't think it would be appropriate for me to continue my efforts. I felt the town needed to heal and wouldn't be ready for such an undertaking.

Mayor Joel Gill was my only contact in Holmes County, which is the most obese county in America. Riding on the edge of the Delta Region, it's an eight-town county, Pickens being one of them. I had coordinated my efforts with him, and he'd welcomed my visit with open arms. He expressed jubilance with a desperate plea, hoping this might be the change the community needed; someone from the outside, bringing a different perspective and experience.

When he mentioned his town is nearly one-hundred percent diabetic, and when he did, I sensed embarrassment in his tone, but with acceptance. It seemed like an uninhabitable environment, only made me more curious to how these people lived. I knew it was a challenging task ahead of me, and I wasn't so sure I could do it alone.

I understand the fundamentals of coaching, having trained professional and collegiate athletes in various sports, and competing at a high level myself, but the nutritional aspect was more than I could chew. With extensive research,

I reached out to a few qualified dietitians, nutritionists and health gurus, asking if they wanted to join my efforts.

In the same week as Mayor Gill's death, both nutritionists, who showed initial excitement, withdrew from visiting Mississippi. They assured me that the project was incredibly commendable, but they were a bit more fearful of the situation. I don't know too many people who would leave the comfort of their home, just for the sake of a good cause. Though it seemed like I was embarking on failure, I was determined to make a change and a long-lasting impression in this community. My purpose grew.

I dedicated the month of November to the town's health and wellness. With that, in the first night's meeting, I gave the twelve participants five goals that would help them with their daily practices.

1) If your destination is under one mile, walk.
2) Drink the recommended 6-8 glasses of water per day, which could help replace the unhealthier drink consumption, ie. Soda, sweet tea.
3) Take the stairs instead of the elevator, which shouldn't be much of a challenge in the area.
4) Park your car furthest away from the entrance of your destination
5) Never exercise alone. Bring your friend, neighbor, or co-worker with you. This was a way to build a support system.

After the hour-long meeting and detailing my visit timeline, I told everyone that I'd see them for our first workout in the morning. To my surprise, they wanted to start that night. I hadn't planned a workout, but since they were novice walkers and joggers, I knew I could come up with something. Learning about the limited resources they had in Pickens, I was pleasantly relieved the town had a lit walking track. The rough, curvy terrain, mostly unmaintained with roots reaching out of the asphalt, became our nightly meeting spot.

As we breezed—well at least a few of us—around the track for 35 minutes, I had the chance to meet everyone and learn their goals. Many of them just wanted to lose weight and look and feel better about themselves while others wanted to have more energy throughout the day and to learn how to be healthier and more active. Some had a stronger purpose.

"I want to be an example for my daughter. I can barely buckle my seatbelt," one lady mentioned.

"I just lost my husband, which has been a huge wake up call," another expressed.

My goal was to get them excited and make them care to change by using these examples to fuel their energy and motivation.

Back at the church, Rev. William's sermon focused on the importance of health, realizing that my visit may have influenced the morning.

"The Bible says, thou shall not abuse their body," he said to his flock. "Your body is precious, and it's un-Godly not to take care of it. Never take it for granted."

It was a powerful message, especially coming from the fittest person in the room, who coincidentally just relocated to Mississippi from Los Angeles for the position. Moving the attention away from himself, the Reverend asked me to say a few words. Instead of speaking from the middle of the isle, with members in front and behind me, I went up near the pulpit. I tried to be calm, but my voice was as shaky as my legs.

"Welcome everybody, I guess you should be welcoming me, since I'm new in town," I blurted out, realizing that was probably the worst way to gain this audience's attention. However, I still got some chuckles, so I boldly continued.

"I've come to Pickens to get your community in action. I came here voluntarily, for the goodness of making a difference in ways I know how. I have a passion for running and the many benefits it brings. I'm so grateful everyone has welcomed me, but we need more people to get involved with this effort. We need this to be a healthy community and work together. See, inspiration is reciprocal. You'll inspire me if I'm inspiring you."

My introduction earned me an "Amen," from the crowd, specifically from many who I'd met that first night.

"We are meeting at three different times of the day, so there are no excuses of being busy," I continued. "So, I hope to see you all there in preparation for the town's first-ever 5k run."

Though my initial intention was to host a 10k; it was obvious the challenge of a 5k was more than enough for the many participants, who'd never exercised recreationally or competitively in their lives. Add in that they only had a month to prepare, needless to say it was a test. Apparently, my short speech was effective, prompting the Reverend himself to rise and yell out to the crowd.

"I will be there," he said loudly. "Let's all take advantage of this opportunity that our community has been given."

For the next hour, the energetic and animated Reverend Williams preached from the Bible, explaining how detrimental hateful words can be.

"Sticks and stones may break my bones, but words could never hurt me," he said. "We've all heard that before, right? Well, it couldn't be more untrue." Watch what you say! Don't say anything that could be hurtful, because nothing is more powerful than the tongue of the devil. Your hurtful words could cause someone into depression, eating disorders, and even suicide."

After church, the acting Mayor, Rayfield Washington, asked if I wanted to come over for lunch and watch the Dallas Cowboys game, promising his wife, Pat, cooked me up some good ole' Southern cooking from scratch. The day before, he took me to Meridian, a larger town located forty miles south because I wanted to try an all-you-can-eat local buffet. Ironically, I wanted to fatten up while trimming everyone else down. I have been slender my entire life and wanted to see how the food would affect me, if at all.

Mayor Washington, an electrician, father of three, and an aspiring Reverend had a heart of gold. Thus far he'd been a dedicated participant and only male who signed up for my workout sessions. After agreeing to lunch, we walked across the street to his house, a newly remodeled home he built himself. I can tell he's highly ambitious and wants the best for his family. His lush lawn, flourishing rose garden, and flawless winding brick walkway didn't' quite fit the mold of the neighborhood.

Next to his two-story, five-bedroom home, which had a separate game and workout room, was a green trailer parked in a dirt lot. Rather than a lush lawn and flowers, the trailer had a three-foot hole in front of it, which was used as a fire pit. Surrounding the pit were almost two dozen people, sitting in plastic lawn chairs and on deflated basketballs. Though these were Mayor Washington's neighbors, it was obvious they were worlds apart.

"Ya, I don't let my kids over there," he said. "They're a different kind of people. They sit around all day. At any given time, they pack up to 25 people to live there. They make more money by not doing anything."

He was referring to government assistance checks they'd receive versus the cost of committing to a low-income job.

I could sense he was fed up with his neighbors and may have had a contentious history with them.

On the other side of the road, there was another trailer converted into a convenience store. Old wooden stairs leading up to a dilapidated swinging front door. Just by the sight of it, I decided not to explore it. But next to Mayor Washington, I felt safe since everyone knew him.

As we walked into his home, I heard his wife yelling the food was ready. The dining room table looked like it was set for Thanksgiving.

"This is all for you," Rayfield says.

As his wife, described the dishes, I was in awe, thinking of how hospitable people can be. Later, Rayfield opened up to me and mentioned how he really appreciated my visit and my concern for his community. His entire family had lived in Pickens for generations, with many of his family members involved with local politics.

"I have never let a person, outside of my family, into my home," he said seriously.

"I'm the first white person then?" I replied. "Man. This means a lot to me."

We sat down to black-eyed peas, macaroni and cheese, biscuits, fried chicken, baked chicken, sweet potatoes, and mashed potatoes, all of which I scarfed down. My stomach was bigger than my eyes. It felt like I could barely walk across the room to get a glass of water. One of Rayfield's teenage boys offered to get me a glass but returned with sweet tea.

"This is all incredible, and it doesn't seem that bad for you, but what do I know?" I said, adding that's why I asked a health guru known as "The Food Babe," from North Carolina to soon join me in Mississippi to prepare diet plans for the community. As a lifelong runner, I've been used to eating anything.

"Mom, could you get me some sugar for the mac' and cheese?" Rayfield's son asked.

"Now, I know that's bad," I said.

Rayfield had to run over to his sickly mother's home, in order to get her to bed. He'd been gone for a while, but I struck up some good sports talk with his kids. I was bragging about how I used to play basketball, but they didn't believe me, so we had to take it outside.

It was humid out, and I wasn't dressed for the occasion, still in my 'church clothes'. After playing a few rounds, I had to bare my white chest just to cool off. As the day turned into night, the sound of the basketball hitting the concrete continued for at least an hour or two.

I realized this side of the tracks was restless, compared with where I was staying. I felt more at ease on the other side of town, where people are safely in their homes. Here, people were strolling the streets, biking one-handed with a can of pop in the other while cars whizzed by staring at us. There are not many outlets along the neighborhood streets, so everyone knew each other passing through.

It was getting late, and Saddie was probably wondering where I was, which prompted me to leave. Time flew by. What was supposed to be an hour-long after-church meal turned to ten hours later Rayfield driving me back to Saddie's with a sack full of food on my lap in his Mercedes SUV, a luxury obviously earned by his hard work.

When Rayfield drove through the streets that evening, it reminded me of searching for Saddie's home in the dark fog when I first arrived. The sky was pitch black with no light pollution or reflective road signs. I remember hoping I would arrive at a decent, or at least comfortable, place. Too my surprise, I arrived at a 12,000 square-foot former plantation, with stunning high ceilings and massive rooms so big it seemed it took a power plant to heat the space.

Living in the home was Richard, Saddie's longtime husband and Ashlei, her seventeen-year-old niece. I had no idea that they were a black family until the evening I arrived on their doorstep. I'd called their house a week prior to thank them for their generous offer. I later learned that Ashlei, studying to attend a local community college, lived in various states from Michigan to Georgia, where her mother resided. Ashlei's mother was planning to visit Pickens later in the week, but for now, it was just Saddie and Ashlei sitting in the kitchen.

Though I'd been given a key, they assured me when I got there, they were always up late chatting. Even though I was ready to hit the sack, I sat down respectfully, thankful there was a television parked on top of the refrigerator, which came in handy during awkward silent moments.

"How was Rayfield's?" Saddie asked.

"Well, I was the first white person to step into his house," I said spiritedly.

"Hahaha, you stupid!" Ashlei said playfully before asking if I'd ever stayed with a black family while traveling across the country.

"Are we your favorite?" she asked, following the question with the boldest of statements. "I bet you're gonna fall in love with a black girl."

"You guys are the first, and of course you're my favorite," I replied.

Holmes County and almost all of Pickens is African American. People were friendly and I started to feel comfortable there.

"Well, I should get to bed since the first group meeting is at 7 a.m.," I suggested.

Saddie said she hoped to be there on time, but taking her husband Richard to dialysis, which was 70 miles each way, as early as 5 a.m. and returning on time to change may make it impossible.

"If not, Ashlei and I will be there tomorrow night," she said.

My delightful hosts, Saddie, Ashlie and her mother
before deep-frying our Thanksgiving turkey.

After saying good night, I went to my room, consisting of a king size bed with an old antique frame. I stood by the furnace and planned the week's training regimen. The temperature was rapidly dropping, and I wasn't sure how many people would actually show up, but I was prepared for the twelve who attended the first meeting.

My alarm was irrelevant, having been up all night envisioning the weeks ahead that lead to the day of the 5k. As soon as the sun rose, I got dressed and walked to the courthouse, where our morning sessions met.

Rayfield was standing there ready and waiting, already anxious to get moving. He wore warm-up pants and a white sweatshirt to go with his white 1970's walking shoes.

"Do you have any other shoes than those," I asked for the sake of preventing injury.

"Why, these no good?" he asked.

"They're okay for today, but once we start putting miles in, I would get some running shoes," I suggested.

While we stood there waiting for the rest of the crew, Rayfield mentioned his wife and cousin were on their way.

"Thanks for having me over last night, it was a day to remember," I expressed.

Rayfield began to blush, showing off his fondness for our newfound friendship.

"Yeah man, did you try that banana pudding that I sent you home with?" he asked.

"That was insane," I replied.

"My mom made that for you."

Pat and Delores, Rayfield's cousin, show up a few minutes late, which was not acceptable by my policy. We hurried into the stretches before I gave them the workout of the day. I joined them for a casual walk around town. While walking down the side of the highway, residents honked their horns, asking if we needed rides.

"Why you guys walking?" one gentleman yelled in sarcasm.

It was obvious how the people around you can either pick you up or bring you down, but all progress is made by doing things unreasonable.

"Let's head up that little hill." I directed the group down a street along the cemetery.

"Little hill?" Delores expressed. "You crazy, that ain't no little hill."

"Just go your own pace," I advised. "We only have three weeks until our race, don't worry, you're not gonna die."

"Hmm, smells like someone's frying some chicken," Delores observed.

She was right. It smelled good the further we traveled up the hill. Crisco was the scent of the town, maybe the state, as I was reminded of my arrival at the Jackson, Mississippi Airport terminal and Saddie's kitchen. The smell sticks to your clothes like the smoke from cigarettes.

"We're gonna have to stay away from that, huh Daniel?" Dolores asked wittily. "I'm tryin' to look good. Maybe we should get ourselves into a fashion show."

"I heard they have one at the prison," Pat mentioned.

"Oh, they'll be doing more time when they see me," Delores said laughing.

Delores was a character, always smiling, laughing, and telling jokes. But motivated she was. Her goal was to lose 60 pounds, so she could look like she did 20 years ago. It was obvious she needed people to workout with, so she didn't feel so alone. And I really wanted to help her. We headed back after a 35-minute walk, and I told them to keep stretching to prevent injury and enable muscles to work most effectively.

My next group at noon was much larger. We met outside the town hall building, where I took a few minutes trying to convince the office secretary, Felicia to join us.

"Maybe tomorrow," she suggested.

"But I know you got dressed for today," I replied.

"My knees are sore," she said. "I will come out tomorrow."

I could tell she didn't want to embarrass herself in front of the group of eight outside the door. Felicia was well over 300 pounds, and I knew it wasn't where she wanted to be.

"Just come outside, get some fresh air during your lunch break," I pushed.

Felicia was the heaviest of the group, but I knew she could serve as the town's inspiration. I quickly decided to privately call over one of the participants and ask if they could walk alongside Felicia for 20 minutes. Her name was Ursula, a very young looking seventy-year-old who was morbidly overweight herself. I wanted them to form a partnership and hold one another accountable.

The noon participants learn how to stretch
their calves as our warmup

At that moment, a cell phone rung. It was a call from one of the neighbors, mentioning another health-related death in the community. This was the reality of Pickens, but I knew it could be prevented.

"You've got to get Felicia moving," I told Ursula.

Within the first two workout sessions, I learned the layout of Pickens. The main drag was Route 64, the quintessential American highway complete with a courthouse, library, hardware store, and a police station. A few streets over, is the more decrepit part of downtown, which had been making a comeback in the last few decades with a local bank, post office, and a daycare center. Further up the hill with an occasional occurrence of blowing cotton like tumbleweed, you can find a Family Dollar and Piggly Wiggly. The churches are within the residential part of town, directly off Route 64.

However, what the town was missing were its original schools and gyms, town staples that once thrived. That's where the sign of the times is obvious. All Pickens youth attend schools in different towns, and much of the community commutes to work. The town once flourished with the papermill, which employed thousands, but now the building is nothing more than a historical site due to monopolizing corporations and lower manufacturing costs elsewhere.

With the local economy shift of near nothing, Pickens is just a sleeping town, making its residents drive further and further to work, and sit longer and longer in a car spending time and money on what could've been used for healthier lifestyle choices, like eating better and having more time to exercise.

With no team sports in Pickens or the nearby communities, parents must make a commitment to travel out of town to get their children involved. And quite frankly, there are just too many miles between towns.

Although health and poverty are intricately linked, I was in Pickens to prove what could be done with limited resources and a harsh environment, overcome by will, self-determination and developing good habits.

I knew Saddie would be a large part of the solution, and she proved me right when her and Ashlei showed up at the track at 7 p.m. just like she said. The two lined up with six others, including Rayfield AGAIN, who truly cared to learn, and help be an example of change. As we did the first night under the lit track, we walked for almost forty minutes to get their bodies adjusted to moving that long. A pesky barking dog that we couldn't tell if it was tied or not, kept some of us from venturing to one side of the track.

"This week will be moderate," I told the group. "Just make sure you're stretching often at home, drinking water, and you don't cheat yourself."

After a week, I wasn't satisfied with just twelve participants, and Saddie sensed it. I visited her at the library to discuss how to attract more people when a large lady walked in to return books.

"Hey there, Mrs. Richards," Saddie called out. "Have you heard about the Turkey Trot 5k and all the prepping we're doing for it?"

"No, what's that about?" she replied.

Saddie gave her the rundown of workout times and locations, along with the road race.

"Okay, I'll be there if I'm not sleeping," she confirms.

"Want me to wake you up?" Saddie pressures.

"No, it's okay," Mrs. Richards said.

"How about them?" I asked Saddie, pointing to a group of white elders sitting around a table having a discussion over coffee and cake.

"Why don't you go over and introduce yourself?" she said.

So I did. I explained what I was trying to do for the community, and they agreed to participate.

They never showed up.

So, I printed flyers and walked door-to-door to every business. The hardware supply owner was a very large, thick bearded white man.

"Want to participate?" I asked him.

"Oh no, but I'll drive alongside you guys," he said in all seriousness.

Later in the day, I met his brother, whose sad excuse for not participating was due to the world ending.

"What's the point?" he asked as serious as his brother.

As I continued to do outreach, I was getting interesting responses to the 5k participation.

"Can you offer a one-mile fun run?" and "My blood pressure is lower than those that exercise, so I don't know about that!"

I lost patience when one lady responded that she'd do it, but came up with multiple excuses for her stubborn husband that would refuse any direction from me.

"Okay, not my loss!" I responded.

But two weeks later to my total surprise, a friend of a friend, neighbor of a neighbor, and family member of a family member began showing up to my workout sessions. Between the quality workouts, contagious enthusiasm, and total commitment, the workouts struck like wildfire all because of the initial twelve participants. The challenge for the newcomers was that they had to train at an accelerated pace. My lunchtime group consisted of eighteen people, all black females.

"Today is the day I've been waiting for; hill repeats," I told the group.

After a mile warm up, formally the distance of an entire workout, we reached the base of the hill. There were a few bystanders on both sides of the street quite curious about the pain I was putting my group through.

"Want to join?" I yelled out to a young woman standing there with a child.

She pointed at the kid, signally her hands were tied, and one of my athletes, Rev. Gwendolyn Sample mentioned she was only twelve and that was her baby brother.

Never in a hundred years, would I've have figured she was younger than thirty. She was 5'10, around 275 pounds. Though her hands were tied, it was obvious she was both interested and intimidated by the group.

"Those are the people we need here," I told Rev. Sample.

Reverend Sample favored my visit from the get-go. She'd tried to attract workout groups because her community suffered from obesity, diabetes, high blood pressure, and health-related deaths. She hosted a fairly successful church walk-a-thon but it just couldn't seem to sustain interest.

"I really don't know much about fitness," she said, adding she just grabbed a group of girls and started walking. "We don't have many resources here; no weight room, treadmills, swimming pools, basketball courts, sidewalks, nothing."

She thanked me for being there, saying I was making the needed difference in so many lives throughout the community.

"I really love Pickens, this is my home," she said.

She needed to lose weight herself, along with her two children, who were being led directly down the wrong path by their unhealthy mother. Ursula and Felicia were ahead but were struggling on the hill. However, they were carrying 20 pounds less than a few weeks earlier. Their bodies were proof to the rest that exercising and eating healthy can turn you into a different person.

"I can't go back down that hill, I'm gonna roll down," Felicia said exhausted.

Don't get me wrong. She wasn't complaining. In fact, she never complained, which constantly impressed me. Felicia doesn't know it, but her strong will and undying effort kept me going when I started to weaken as a coach.

Meanwhile, The Food Babe, aka Vani, was a few days away from joining me in Pickens. I asked her to visit after finding her popular blog. I mentioned I needed help educating the community and asked for assistance in a number of ways.

First, I wanted to develop a weekly meal plan that would gradually improve their eating habits with less portions and healthier choices. Though not a licensed nutritionist, I knew shocking their systems with foreign foods would discourage them to change.

Second, I asked her to educate the community on what's in their food and how they should really start paying attention to what they eat. I specifically wanted them to recognize how what they eat affects their health, attitude, and energy level.

Third, I felt it was important to understand strict budget. I encouraged Vani to learn what their constraints were while getting to know them on a personal level so she could help them cut specific costs.

I told her it would be important to find out each participant's daily routine including work, school, church, etc. Too often the excuse to not being healthier is due to lack of time or resources. Granted, some may not have proper cookware, or cars to access the grocery store.

I told Vani they needed help with shopping since Pickens had the most basic grocery store with nothing fresh. Though there was another store almost 40 miles away, I thought it would be good for the group to work with what they had, making the best of their local resources. I knew she could help them find or create healthy recipes that didn't include many ingredients or supplies. Ideally, I suggested she help them save money by cutting out their junk food purchases.

Lastly, I asked her to offer tips on food related to exercise, specifically on what to eat before and after a workout to keep their energy level up. What types of fluids should they be drinking and what they should be cutting? But most of all, I shared with her how important the emotional state of the community was and how to get them excited to learn first and change second. I ended my email saying it was important for us to find leaders who could help guide their community in the right direction, especially when we left. We had to create a team environment for everyone to support and feed off one another.

Upon Vani's arrival, I asked the group members to take advantage of her visit by signing up for a one-on-one session. With the 5k so close, excitement was growing. Only four days left until the big event, which I got Piggly Wiggly to sponsor, supplying post-race food and drink. Everything was coming together, and I couldn't have been more ecstatic. But then I noticed I had a voicemail.

"Daniel, can you come to the Mayor's office?" Rayfield asked.

A pit grew in my stomach, something didn't sound right in his tone. I rushed over to the office where the office staff, Rayfield, and three town elders refused to look me in the eyes.

"Sit down, Daniel," Mayor Rayfield said. "We have some bad news."

I looked around the room again, but still nobody could make eye contact with me. There was no emotion on their face. Rayfield handed me a print out of Vani's blog post:

Visiting the World's Most Obese Place

After I read the title, I looked up at him.

"We know we're the fattest county in America, we know we're the fattest country in the world," he said boldly. "We know that makes us known to be the fattest people on the planet. We know this! But you've made a mockery of us Daniel. I know this probably wasn't your intention, but we're hurt. The entire town is hurt."

I sat motionless.

"Rev. Sample is too hurt to continue this 5k race," he continued. "She's pulling out and so is the Piggly Wiggly sponsorship."

I took a deep breath, leaned back in my chair and asked to read the post.

Pickens is located in a food desert.......

It wasn't good, none of it was positive.

"Look, I have no part of this," I said. "I can't control what she thinks or writes, and we've worked too hard this month. We can't let this stop us."

All of the sudden, I remembered Rev. William's sermon my first Sunday in town about how powerful and evil the tongue can be. How he preached hurtful words could destroy a community. He was right. It was literally before my eyes.

"Look, I'm gonna have a talk with her and ask her to take it down," I told them.

When I called Vani that night, I was caught between the insensitive truth and a community attempting to protect itself.

"You're in for a big treat," I said. "The entire town is on edge because of your post."

"I'm getting on the plane tomorrow, should I not come?" Vani asked.

"I think you should still come," I said, adding her rebound back to the community trusting her may be hard and she'd have to explain herself. "This is your passion."

I had returned my rental car weeks ago, leaving myself vulnerable in the town of Pickens. I couldn't escape even if I wanted. Police Chief Davis offered me a ride to the airport to pick up Vani. Once there, she and I would share a rental car for the weekend.

Small town chatter in the Pickens, Mississippi police station. From right to left, (Delores, Rayfield, Officer Joe and his colleague)

When jumping into Chief Davis's police car, I noticed a wandering vagabond strolling into town on foot. It was young black girl with just a backpack who looked really frightened.

"Where are you coming from?" Davis asked.

She didn't really give an answer, but the Chief found that she walked from Jackson, a good 65 miles away.

"We'll give you a ride back to the city," he offered.

Though she got in the backseat, she immediately changed her mind and got out.

"Does that happen often?" I asked Davis.

"We have some strange stuff coming through town sometimes," he replied.

There I was cruising down the interstate with Chief Davis, distracted by his Big Gulp and bag of chips. We stopped at a drive-thru, even though he mentioned not being hungry.

"Do you want anything?" he asked.

"I'll just get a cup of water," I replied.

He handed me pink lemonade.

"So, what do you think of this whole blog thing?" I asked.

"I'm not from Pickens, but I know they have a problem," he said. "What was written was true, so I didn't see anything wrong with it."

"You think we'll still have this race?" I asked.

"Oh yeah, they'll get over it," he said.

"Do you like running?" I asked, knowing he'd say no.

"Oh no, haha. I do like hunting," he states.

I told the chief I appreciated his help and asked once I figured out the 5k (3.1 mile) course around town, if he would help me block the streets on race day.

"Oh yeah, that won't be a problem," he said.

After riding Vani back to her hotel 40 miles from Pickens, where the concierge greeted her with a bag chips, Vani wanted to prepare for the evening presentation and asked if we could go grocery shopping at Walmart. While she was searching for kale shake ingredients to make a health drink that would surely shock the system and taste buds of my participants, I was crossing my fingers hoping people would show up that night. I especially was hoping Rev. Sample showed since I'd heard she never wanted to see or hear from me again.

At 7 p.m. sharp we started our presentation at the courthouse with a food demonstration, devoting a significant time for questions. Vani was blending her shake, explaining the pure ingredients of it, while I was twitching my feet, wondering where everyone was. People did stroll in late, but it almost felt like my first night in Pickens.

Vani didn't miss a beat, going on with her talk no matter how many people walked in. That was when I saw a guy outside the glass door, peeking in. Rayfield checks the nature of his lurk. My body got sweaty, thinking the worst.

"Are they planning to kill me?" I thought in paranoia.

Maybe the shame I put on the community was worth my life. When Rayfield came back in and asked me to go outside, my paranoia got worse.

"Crap, this is what I was afraid of," I thought.

"Rev. Sample is waiting in the parking lot," Rayfield told me.

I go outside, see headlights in the dark and walk toward them. I was cautious of being jumped, but I was already vulnerable, so I just gave in. There was Rev. Sample, standing beside her car.

"Hey Gwen, you showed up," I said cautiously.

"I'm not going in," she said. "I just wanted to tell you in person that I'm done. I trusted you and you exposed us, just as you said you wouldn't."

I stood there listening since there was nothing I could do to change her mind.

"You broke my heart," she said. "I love my town."

"I didn't mean for this to happen," I said. "Really, I'm sorry."

The disappointment in her eyes pushed out the tears in mine.

"You know I wouldn't do this intentionally; I came here to make a difference," I said. "I hope you'll forgive me and come to the race tomorrow."

"Alright, well I'll sleep on it and see how I feel," she said to my surprise.

I went back into the courthouse filled with raised hands waiting for answers across the room. Vani looked at me, asking with her eyes where I'd been. It seemed the audience was more curious about their health than how hurt they were by Vani's blog, which she agreed to temporarily take down.

Before the meeting dismissed, Mayor Rayfield asked to go over the 5k race route.

"I hope everyone gets a good night's rest, because you're all going to need it," he said to the crowd. "This is the longest any of us have ever run."

My goal was for everyone to finish, but if most of them could run without stopping, I would consider that a bonus. We went over the race route one more time, and as we did, you could sense Rayfield's enthusiasm through his animation of directions.

"8AM, we're all going to meet at the MLK community center. We're going to go one lap around the track, go a half lap and then out by Mrs. Jacob's house. You're going to go all the way down by Mrs. MacDonald's house, get on the highway and run on the shoulder of the road. Come back around and pass Mrs. MacDonald's house again. This time you're going through downtown, cross over the train tracks and up the hill by the cemetery. Once you get on the top of the hill, you can see the Promised Land--(MLK center). You're not going to go over there. You can look over there, but you're not done yet. You must come back down the hill on the other side of downtown, cross back on the highway and back through the neighborhoods. After about a half mile, you're going to reach the Promised Land, but you're not done yet. You must go around them cones we'll have set up. Come around and pass the tree and that's 3.1 miles."

I couldn't sleep the night before the race. I was too excited, anxious, and concerned that everything wouldn't go as planned. As soon as I got up from not sleeping, I went to the Piggly Wiggly to pick up our sponsored supplies including bananas, oranges, cereal snacks, and water.

I wasn't surprised that Rev. Sample didn't pull her connections at Piggly Wiggly, who promised sponsorship before Vani's blog post. I knew she wouldn't want to sabotage her town's health no matter how personally hurt she may be.

I picked up three turkeys, one each for the best male, female and participant who gave the best effort. After, I went to the library to get tables for water and then to the police station to get cones to mark the course.

"Don't worry Dan, we're gonna have a lot of people," Rayfield assured me.

Thirty minutes before the race started, the parking lot was dusty as a windstorm with all the cars rolling in. There wasn't even enough room for the finish line, so we had to move it, which was a pleasant hindrance for sure.

One participant surprised me by making nearly seventy numbered bibs, one for each competitor. When I looked out at the line of participants, I was amazed by what was before me. The gathering was all by choice—nobody forced me, nobody forced them. It's amazing what can be done with leadership, with community, with purpose.

Between the balloons hanging from the fence, the smiling faces of the town, and the police cars blocking the streets, I was pumped. Rayfield called everyone into a circle for prayer.

"We are strengthened by God to be here," he said fervently. "We are very thankful for giving our town the opportunity to have Daniel open our eyes to wellness."

I grabbed the wristwatch from Rayfield and asked everyone to take their places. With my whistle, the group spurred off at a casually conservative pace. I stood there to observe the first lap, hoping congestion wasn't a factor for those competing and others running for a good time.

As they made their way into the neighborhood streets, I followed closely while assuring the water stations were full. I realized I wasn't the only one cheering the participants, as neighbors came out of their homes and played music from cars.

"I can't believe this is real," I said to one of the bystanders.

Within 30 minutes, the front runners were coming through the finish line. The winner was Felicia's thirteen-year-old son, second a ten-year-old boy, and third was Rayfield.

I went back on the course, looking for Felicia and Ursula. They were both at the halfway mark, considering giving up.

"This is not going to happen today, I'm going with you the rest of the way," I told them as we went on.

As we walked up the toughest part of the course, the hill along the cemetery, we could hear the music playing from the finish line. Unfortunately, the promised land was a mile away. Chief Davis rolled up alongside us, keeping the streets closed while he encouraged us with the song "Eye of the Tiger," from the police car intercom.

As we winded through the final half mile, Felicia's husband ran up to us excited as ever.

"Our son won!," he yelled. "He got us a turkey tonight."

Felicia's pace quickened as the finish line was in sight. Then she started sprinting.

"What the heck," I thought, not believing my eyes.

It's amazing how there's always some driving force and energy reserved with a little inspiration. The crowd was waiting by the line and somehow found a ribbon to hold up as Felicia crossed; her hands in the air with the accomplishment of a community on her back.

Crowd goes wild, as Felicia's doubt of finishing vanishes.

Just a few seconds behind, Ursula got the same blue-ribbon treatment. After the race, we all circled around Rayfield, who encouraged everyone to continue what they've learned. At that moment, I felt my genuine effort to build a healthier community was a success. Then I gave the last turkey away.

"I wanted to give out the award for the best effort during the month of November," I said to the crowd. "We've become close friends. He's been coming to workouts almost three times a day and he's been one of my inspirations for continuing this effort. The turkey goes to Rayfield Washington."

So I thought until he whispered in my ear to give it to Ursula.

"Rayfield has asked for me to give the award to Ursula, who has impressed all of us," I said to the crowd.

Surrounded by a bunch of colored balloons tied to a turkey, Ursula blushed before the crowd. She said she was grateful to have an opportunity to run her first road race, and went from complaining about her asthma and being overweight, to accomplishing a feat she'd never guess she could.

I left the following day with Vani, who agreed with me that the experience was both rewarding and powerful. We both planned on staying in touch with the community.

Fast forward six months. I got a call from Rayfield Washington.

"Daniel, guess who's the mayor now?" he asked laughing.

"I know, Saddie told me that you won in a landslide," I said. "That's no surprise."

"We are still training daily, and even added another workout session in the mid-afternoon," he said with pride. "We also have an aerobics class in the courtroom on Tuesday nights."

"Looks like you guys don't need me anymore," I said.

"You're welcome to Pickens anytime!" Rayfield said.

Midwest's Troubles

$\mathcal{I}$ was heading north from Mississippi to the industrial cities of the upper Midwest, just as millions had to find work during the Great Migration.

I arrived in Chicago, late winter, ready to understand a community we only hear tragic stories about on the news. I sat in my rental car at a stop sign, deep on the southside of the city. I gazed up to see which street I was on and found myself at 103rd, also known as the Wild 100s. I felt uneasy knowing the higher the street number, the further away from downtown and the more crime ridden the neighborhood was.

As expected, it was a world apart from the glamour of Michigan Avenue's Miracle Mile—grassy vacant lots, and decrepit brick buildings, some with a red 'x' sign marked as condemned. I try to imagine myself living in the most notorious gang-infested community in America. Some even nickname the city, Chi-raq, a place more people have been shot and killed than in the war in Iraq. Taking in the scene, I saw the stereotype roll right by me; a 1988 Cadillac DeVille with five young black men cruising around, unfazed. Some of them wearing black knit caps, others with scruffy beards, but all wore stoic faces. A cigarette dangled from the driver's lips with his seat reclined far back, one of his arms fully extended to reach the top of the steering wheel. Just as I was looking at the rear end of their car, I had déjà vu from my time in Eastern Kentucky of hillbillies of the Appalachian Mountains; same car, different demographic in a different setting. Intimidation was the game. Pride and respect were the purpose, even if that meant using a gun.

Much of America is cursorily acquainted with the 'streets', whether it's from making a wrong turn or what they've seen or heard from the mainstream media. The 1991 blockbuster hit film, *Boyz N the Hood* comes to mind, which depicted the reality of the streets of South-Central Los Angeles. At the time, it was the most dangerous quarter in the country, including the surrounding communities of Compton, Inglewood, and Watts, where gangster rap was founded. There were many noteworthy and thought-provoking scenes from the movie that made it such a hit. Laurence Fishburne's character enlightened a few young thugs with his question, "Why do you think there's a liquor store on every street corner in this neighborhood? The same reason why there's a gun shop on every corner in this neighborhood. They want us to kill ourselves." We find this theme all too familiar throughout the inner cities, and although Chicago has some of the strictest gun laws in the country, we realized from the dry reservation in South Dakota, if there's a demand, there'll be a supply.

Opportunities are scarce. There is nothing to keep the youth occupied, and like in this film, many young people are roving the streets or hanging out on their porch, while the single mother is out trying to support the large family. The statistics are real. When it comes to the death of young black men, one out of every twenty-one will be murdered by another black man. I wanted to learn what was going on in the 'hood and whether there was hope of stopping the vicious cycle, at least for an individual.

I've seen Los Angeles reasonably progress, since the release of *Boyz N the Hood*. Just under fifteen years later, I found myself in the same neighborhood as a student of The University of Southern California, also known as University of South Central. I didn't like it. Each time I left campus, I always felt anxious on my mile walk home, more so at night. USC's school colors are cardinal red, a similar color to the infamous Blood gang, so if the opposing gang, Crips mistook me, I was a target.

One night, I was walking home from a campus function. I took a new route, coming from a different part of campus. My eyes wide open on high alert, head constantly turning, as the streets were unusually quiet. The only sounds I heard were dogs' metal collars clinking as they paced back and forth through the front yards. I saw an old vehicle a few blocks down the street blaring music and driving towards me. They shut off their lights and stereo and started creeping closer. My heart skipped a beat and then burst into rapid fire. It was a straight mimic from a scene out of *Boyz N the Hood*, where a promising athlete was gunned down running through an alley. I took off running down a side street, as they started chasing me. Hearing the screech of their wheels, I was able to assess where they were. I jumped over a ten-foot wall in one motion spurred on by adrenaline and avoided an eventful night.

Considering this took place only a week after I moved to Los Angeles, I wanted to transfer. What they wanted from me I will never know. Life is unpredictable in the streets. You never know what sets someone off.

We hear tragic stories across the nation of gang violence and innocent bystanders, most commonly in South Chicago. In 2006, a year after graduating from college, I found myself in Chicago, where I worked as a volunteer coach at Northwestern University for the women's cross-country team. One of the first things I noticed about the city was the distinction between the north and south. On clear display, if you ride south on the redline of the Chicago "L" train, you can observe at the Roosevelt stop, where the whites get off and the blacks gets on. I never dared to go further south because of the drastic and dreary change in scenery, but there was always this curiosity.

Flash forward a few years later in my coaching career, I earned the head coaching position at a prestigious middle school, The Laboratory Schools, where President Obama's children attended, located in Hyde Park. This neighborhood is an anomaly to the Southside of Chicago, namely because of the notable institution, The University of Chicago.

We didn't have many places to practice other than a grass field across the street from the school's entrance. Luckily, it was a large enough to use and have decent workouts and a neighborhood security guard within sight. Half of my athletes were black from the local area, while the white athletes were driven in. One of my athletes had a personal chauffeur, that's because it was Mayor of Chicago Rahm Emanuel's daughter.

The team was well behaved, very studious, and decent athletes. What was important to me was that they were respectful and disciplined. Looking deep into the relationships of the team, the good athletes hung out with the good athletes, and the social athletes hung out with the social athletes. Surprisingly, it wasn't separated by race. I applaud the school for creating such an atmosphere, where students blended based on interests.

The train ride was often scary. The bus ride was often scary. I never tried making eye contact with anyone, hoping not to attract attention. There were always passengers cutting through the train carts, looking for trouble. Any given time, you'd find a church minister tabling near the ticket machines, hoping to save a young soul. It's an understandable effort, because if the parent can't be a positive role model or the teacher can't engage their student's interest, then the gangs prey on the vulnerable and gain power. Gangs have been a part of Chicago's long history, and its origins developed as different ethnic groups provided protection against one another.

If you've wondered how blacks ended up in cold climate cities like Detroit, Cleveland, St. Louis, Milwaukee, and Chicago, it's because of job opportunities that they couldn't find in the rural Southern states. In the early to mid-1900's, approximately 6 million blacks sacrificed their long history and culture in the South to move north to make a new living. This was known as The Great Migration. They found jobs but still couldn't escape segregation. Factory employers only hired the new migrants if they agreed to live in certain neighborhoods, which became known as the "Black Belt". This was a prime example and era of institutional racism. Over time, low-skilled Europeans laborers settled into the same neighborhoods, and gangs started to form.

Neighborhood dwellings started to overcrowd, and homes deteriorated. The jobs in the factories and stockyards that the blacks migrated for were disappearing. As blacks lived below the poverty line, the federal government stepped in to build affordable housing. The high-rise housing projects were built to accommodate tens of thousands of families of mostly black residents. Martin Luther King visited Chicago to protest segregated housing and was physically attacked by much of the white community. In 1968, riots erupted over his death and that segregated the city even further, causing whites to flee the southside and westside of Chicago, only to leave blacks in destroyed neighborhoods and the newly developed housing projects.

This created a separate society; one that grew dejected, isolated, and dependent. The chemistry of a concentrated community of unskilled, uneducated, and impoverished concocted the ultimate disaster of a hopelessness. Some theorize that this was the intention of the government. Social welfare programs after the Civil Rights were generous and numerous and became a way of life, taking away the incentive to work and valuing education.

Historically, welfare was created to provide the freed slaves with the resources to gain footing towards an independent and prosperous future. It made sense then, but why do we still provide welfare in the same capacity as we did hundreds of years ago? Are people claiming to be in as bad condition today as those coming out of slavery? People are naturally adaptable in some of the worst circumstances, but when there's this government support system creating dependency, people won't make the sacrifices they once made, like migrating to where work could be found.

I reached out to the founder of the non-profit organization, Kids of the Block, Diane Latiker. Kids of the Block serves as a safe haven for kids to go to after school instead of being influenced or harmed by gangs. She started this grassroots movement from the comfort of her living room, where she literally invited kids from the neighborhood into her home and gave them a place to stay off the streets. Diane seemed receptive to having me come work with some of her youth, whether it was teaching them how to use computers, tutoring, or sharing my experiences of career exploration.

When I arrived in Chicago, she wasn't available. This became a common theme, my first week in Chicago. Everyone that I had planned to meet or work for, was no longer available, so there I was, halted at the stop sign at 103rd Street trying to figure out how to learn about this gun violence epidemic. It was out of the question to join a gang and experience their life, but I thought I'd at least get exposure to the life by working with an organization dealing with the youth. Reporting on the life of gangs and violence in the 'hoods had been done to death, so I wanted to try a different approach.

I was staying in my friend's apartment downtown, as I was waiting for things to develop, but I still had nothing. I hung out in hotel lobbies and hospitals down his street getting a feel for the neighborhood while hoping someone would call me back. I contacted many of the non-profits, like the YMCA gang-prevention program, Cease Fire, South Chicago Help Center, just to name a few. I showed up to the office of All-Stars Project, a New York City based organization that provides youth with tools to help them succeed in the most devastating environments.

"What are you planning for me to do?" I asked the director.

"We're making cold calls, asking for donations and volunteers right now," she responded.

I wanted to walk out the door, but I respectfully stayed to show my interest in assisting. Making cold calls couldn't have been further from what I was hoping for. I sat there listening to three young adults making scripted calls, sometimes in sync. That day, I found out that All Stars was hosting a talent show, located in Gresham, the most dangerous district in Chicago. That's where I wanted to be, but the event was already in progress.

I was getting nowhere fast in this region. The next morning, I drove to the affluent suburb of Naperville to speak at the local Rotary Club and share my experiences of the previous four regions. I confessed in front of three-hundred audience members that I'd hit the wall in my ability to have an impactful experience in South Chicago.

After the presentation, two members came up and suggested reaching out to their acquaintances. They handed me contact information of police lieutenants and professors of the South Chicago district.

Still frustrated with my lack of success, I gave one of the contacts a call. I didn't know how to introduce myself. I'm not a journalist, nor did I want to approach this as one. I got a hold of Professor Townsend, from Jackson State University, located on the southside. I did ask a series of questions, but he jumped to point out corruption.

"If you take a drive down South State Street, you're going to see more churches than you've seen in your life. They could help the community, but they're just taking people's money." As a professor of cultural affairs, I could hear how frustrated he was with people not working together. Maybe that answered why I had such a difficult time finding an organization to work with.

I did as he suggested, I drove down State Street. It's interesting to observe what problems you can find in a community by what's written on the wall, or in this case a billboard.

Hanging above an abandoned Eastern European sausage company, was a billboard stating the thirty percent high school dropout rate. Everything was decrepit. For Sale signs on schools, vacant factories, bar-windowed homes and convenience stores that became brewing grounds for gang activity; and, on a gloomy cold day, it looked worse. Cops seemed to be in the middle of the street with their lights flashing, on just about every block. I kept going. It was a world I wanted to get intimate with to contemplate the cause and effect.

Police are present on just about every corner in South Chicago.

I went for a drive to the Roseland neighborhood, a long strip of a "downtown" shopping area, but it looked like I came forty years too late. A rare uphill crest of the road gave me a moment to overlook the region. It was a telling glimpse of the area, nothing but endless fifty-foot poles advertising fast food chains, dollar stores, cash advance establishments, laundry mats, and the like that cater to the poor. In many impoverished urban settings, you can't find any food establishments besides fast food or convenient stores, almost a food desert like the Mississippi Delta. The more I drove, the more precarious the situation became. "Was it all in my mind?" I thought. People walking and biking in the middle of the street, making crosswalks obsolete.

I kept going, trying to observe the neighborhoods further. Some residential streets were quite nice, then you go on to the main drag, it's bad again. I approached a construction zone, where they closed one lane. Cones were in place, huge orange signs citing the construction, as I was going over potholes. One oncoming car decided to merge into my lane, passed another and nearly caused a head-on collision with me. They didn't care, they were thugs ruling the streets and drinking while driving.

I pulled over to regroup. This was not working. I needed to be involved.

I went to the Gresham Police Department and asked the sergeant if they would be willing to have me ride-along for a night to observe the crime.

"Are you sure you want to do that here?" he replied.

"Heck yeah!"

After thinking about the potential experience, I didn't want to be riding in a police vehicle observing crime as if it were an exhibit. I'm not interested in covering gangs, rather the way of life and how the lack of unemployment or opportunity causes such havoc.

Instead, I called up the Southside Help Center, whose mission is to help at-risk youth overcome challenges they face by making positive and healthy choices. Like Kids of the Block, the center serves as a safe haven for kids afterschool. I was invited to give a presentation about careers, similar to the one I made on the Pine Ridge Reservation. The director asked all the kids, ages nine to eighteen to come listen to my presentation, otherwise they were doing assignments on computers and chatting as groups of friends.

I was trying to open their eyes to a world outside their own, a seemingly impossible task. It would take a special individual to make it out of the South Chicago projects, one with talent, curiosity, ambition and a non-conformist attitude to do something their peers and family hadn't done. If a student engages in academics, in career and professional development, his or her peers will call them 'soft' or a sellout– part of the White man's system. When O. J. Simpson became a national hero through his talents in athletics and was a poster child for fans across America, the black community called him a sellout and no longer respected him for losing his "black self." How can one excel when your own community brings you down? There's a penalty for success. Then the forces of the government created a system to keep inner city communities down through welfare.

The director wanted to make sure a handful of kids were paying attention. "I can't let you play basketball unless you can list five things about Daniel's talk!"

"Okay, that's easy," one of the kids said eager to prove her doubt.

"He had a difficult time finding a job after graduating from college. He said the toughest job that he worked was making cheese in Wisconsin. He had to adapt to new cultures in each state. He mentioned that meeting strangers on trains, planes, and buses helped him network to find many of his jobs. Lastly, he said that being an athlete helped him work through exhausting times on the road."

This kid remembered the presentation better than the director. It was quite remarkable. I ended up staying another hour, playing basketball, having to improvise to the recently stolen hoop. Universally, sports is the easiest way to relate to most kids, and if you have athletic skills, you gain respect and trust. This was a good group of kids, and it was heart shattering that statistically four out of seven would either end up in jail or be dead by the time they reached twenty-one.

Relating with kids through sports in South Chicago.

"How come kids drop out of school?" I asked the help center director.

"Teen pregnancy, afraid of gangs, feelings of inadequacy, boredom. In this community, it's hard for kids to think long-term and they often have psychological barriers," she said.

While I was waiting on the "L" stop platform at Roosevelt with my luggage, ready to leave the city and finish *Going the Extra Mile*, an elderly black lady with her cane slowly walked towards me and asked me to get out of her way. "Well, son do you speak English? I said move!!" She hit my luggage with her cane and looked at the black man standing right next to me. He nodded at her, like yeah, he's an idiot. I stayed calm, trying to avoid an altercation, but the first thing that came to mind was my grandmother. Not in my wildest dreams could I imagine my grandmother acting like this lady. Maybe that's the problem. If elderly people are aggressive and disrespectful, how is the next generation supposed to turn out? Well, we've found our answer in South Chicago.

Before completing this chapter, I viewed a few 1980's documentaries on Cabrini Green, a notorious Chicago housing project that housed low-income families. Due to its poor planning and managerial neglect, it became a breeding ground for gang recruitment, rape, and drug trafficking. Featured in the opening scene, there was a boy interviewed about how he hears gunfire each day and lives in fear. I decided to look him up and found he was in jail for killing someone. The cycle never ends.

There's one solution, as I'll again refer to the film, *Boyz N the Hood*. You must leave if you want to find a better life. The surviving characters from the film left South Central and went off to college on the East Coast and were able to prosper. There's no shame in wanting to live a better life and working for it.

Maybe I opened a few young minds with my presentation at the help center, but that's not enough. I've decided to sponsor a teen for a trip through several states, to try different jobs and be exposed to a variety of cultures and lifestyles. I want to prove that people can do anything—if they have a vision and exposure to what's possible.

Please follow the journey at www.livingthemap.com

Compassion Breaks Barriers

This journey challenged me. I was out of my element, switching lenses to search for perspective. I temporarily traded my life to learn. I wanted to connect with people, somehow find ways to relate for the purpose of inspiring and empowering lives. At times, it was unfeasible to establish commonalities with those from such drastic backgrounds. There were moments when my wall was up, feeling uncomfortable and uncertain. There were moments when the communities I visited had their walls up, while mine was down. I realized, both walls must come down for meaningful experiences and relationships to exist.

I was just a stranger dropping into town, in which curiosity brought me. What kept me, was the genuine experiences with people. I heard laughter and sorrow from all corners of America. I listened to stories of their past, as we made new ones together.

Learning the challenges of others awakened my compassionate spirit. With that energy, my goal was to make a positive impact. Whether it was getting a Mississippi town moving or opening the minds of kids in Appalachia, I did my best to show that I cared. People can be easily be thought of as a statistic until we come face to face.

What differentiates us is our circumstance and environment, but as Americans our will can unite us. Go the Extra Mile!

CPSIA information can be obtained
at www.ICGtesting.com
Printed in the USA
LVHW032329220920
666848LV00002B/702

9 781735 534688